Magic Lantern Guides

# *Nikon*

# D50

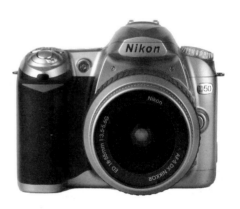

Simon Stafford

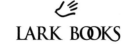

## LARK BOOKS

A Division of Sterling Publishing Co., Inc.
New York

Book Design and Layout: Michael Robertson
Cover Design: Barbara Zaretsky

**Library of Congress Cataloging-in-Publication Data**

Stafford, Simon.
  Nikon D50 / Simon J. Stafford.
      p. cm. -- (Magic lantern guides)
  Includes index.
  ISBN 1-57990-804-7 (pbk.)
  1. Nikon camera--Handbooks, manuals, etc.  2. Digital cameras--Handbooks,
manuals, etc.  3. Single lens reflex cameras--Handbooks, manuals, etc.  I.
Title. II. Series.
TR263.N5S73225 2006
771.3'3--dc22

                                     2005018519

10 9 8 7 6 5 4 3 2

Published by Lark Books, A Division of
Sterling Publishing Co., Inc.
387 Park Avenue South, New York, N.Y. 10016

Distributed in Canada by Sterling Publishing,
c/o Canadian Manda Group, 165 Dufferin Street
Toronto, Ontario, Canada M6K 3H6

Distributed in the United Kingdom by GMC Distribution Services,
Castle Place, 166 High Street, Lewes, East Sussex, England BN7 1XU

Distributed in Australia by Capricorn Link (Australia) Pty Ltd.,
P.O. Box 704, Windsor, NSW 2756 Australia

If you have questions or comments about this book, please contact:
Lark Books
67 Broadway
Asheville, NC 28801
(828) 253-0467

Manufactured in China

ISBN 13: 978-1-57990-804-1
ISBN 10: 1-57990-804-7

For information about custom editions, special sales, premium and corporate purchases, please con-tact Sterling Special Sales Department at 800-805-5489 or specialsales@sterlingpub.com.

Simon Stafford
**Nikon D50**

# Contents

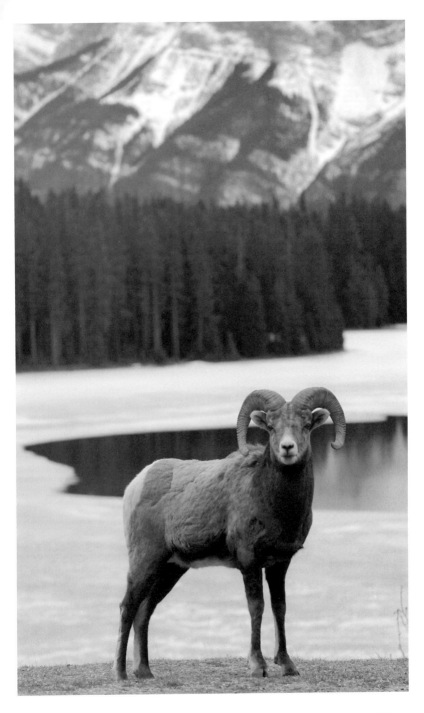

# Introduction

The rapid decline in film camera sales during recent years is a reflection of the exponential growth in popularity of digital cameras. From simple point-and-shoot compact cameras to highly sophisticated professional models, digital cameras have pervaded every level of photography in a very short period of time!

Nikon has a long heritage as an optical engineering company that goes back to the early part of the twentieth century. A decade ago in collaboration with Kodak, Nikon produced high-end digital cameras based on its film cameras. The experience Nikon gained during this period was incorporated into the design of its first independently produced Digital-Single Lens Reflex (D-SLR) camera, the D1, introduced in1999. Since then digital imaging technology has advanced in leaps and bounds and as camera specifications improved the price declined. By early 2004 Nikon was able to introduce the hugely successful D70, which was aimed at the enthusiast photographer. It was the camera that made high-quality Nikon digital photography available at an affordable price. As a measure of its success the D70 has, to date, become the best-selling Nikon SLR ever manufactured.

Nikon's objective with the D50 is to offer a highly capable, feature-laden camera with straightforward handling at a very competitive price point and thereby secure an even more significant share of the demandingly popular D-SLR camera market.

The simplified controls and features such as the fully automatic Vari-program mode are a clear indication of Nikon's aspirations for the D50. These include appealing to the family photographer with little, if any, previous experience of using an SLR type camera. However, by including many features

✍ *Whether you are purchasing a digital SLR for casual family photography or a workshop in the great outdoors, the Nikon D50's smart feature-packed design should be able to handle all of your requirements.*

found on more sophisticated models the camera will also sat-
isfy the needs of more advanced photographers wishing to
exercise a greater level of creative control. Thus, the D50 represents an ideal camera for novice photographers looking to
gain an understanding of fundamental principals, as well as
more advanced users wishing to hone their skills.

## Production of the Nikon D50

It is no coincidence that the D50 is assembled at Nikon's factory in Ayuthaya, just north of Bangkok, Thailand, as this is the
same production facility responsible for the D70, and more
recently its successor the D70s. Between its launch during
March 2004 and the end of its production run a little over
twelve months later over one million D70 cameras where produced, which far exceeded Nikon's original target of 800,000.
To accomplish this phenomenal achievement production was
increased to 90,000 units per month and it is anticipated that
manufacture of the D50 will be no less frenetic!

By sharing the site of production and many core components, such as the same Charge Couple Device (CCD) sensor, Nikon aim to ensure that manufacture of the D50 and
D70s, is both highly efficient and cost effective.

Unlike the D70/70s the D50 is available in two different
finishes, black and silver, and initially the camera will be
supplied with a new Nikon lens the Zoom-Nikkor AF-S DX
18-55mm f/3.5-5.6G ED, also available in the same two finishes to match the camera body.

## Conventions Used In This Book

Unless otherwise stated, when the terms 'left' and 'right' are
used to describe the location of a camera control, it is
assumed the camera is being held to the users' eye in the
shooting position. When referring to a specific Custom Setting, it will sometimes be mentioned in the abbreviated form:

CS-'X' where 'X' is the identifying number of the function. In describing the functionality of lenses and external flash units, it is assumed that appropriate Nikkor lenses and Speedlight units are being used. Note that some early Nikon lenses and flash units or those made by independent manufacturers may function differently. If you use such products, refer to the manufacturers' instruction manuals to check compatibility and operation. If you have any doubts seek advice from an authorised Nikon dealer as use of some incompatible equipment may damage the D50. When referring to Nikon software, it is assumed that Nikon Picture Project (version 1.5.2 or higher, as supplied with the D50), Nikon View (version 6.2.6 or higher, which is available free from Nikon), or the optional Nikon Capture (version 4.3 or higher), is used.

## About This Book

To get the most from your D50 it is important that you understand its features so you can make informed choices about how to use them in conjunction with your style of photography. This book is designed to help you achieve this and should be seen as an adjunct to the camera's instruction manual. Besides explaining how all the basic functions work, this book also provides you with useful tips on operating the D50 and maximizing its performance. The book does not have to be read from cover to cover. You can move from section to section as required, study a complete chapter, or just absorb the principles of the features or functions you want to use.

The key to success, regardless of your level of experience, is to practice with your camera. You do not waste money on film and processing costs with a digital camera; once you have invested in a memory card it can be used over and over again. Therefore, you can shoot as many pictures as you like, review your results almost immediately, and then delete your near misses but save your successes. This trial and error method is a very effective way to learn!

Simon Stafford, Wiltshire, England.

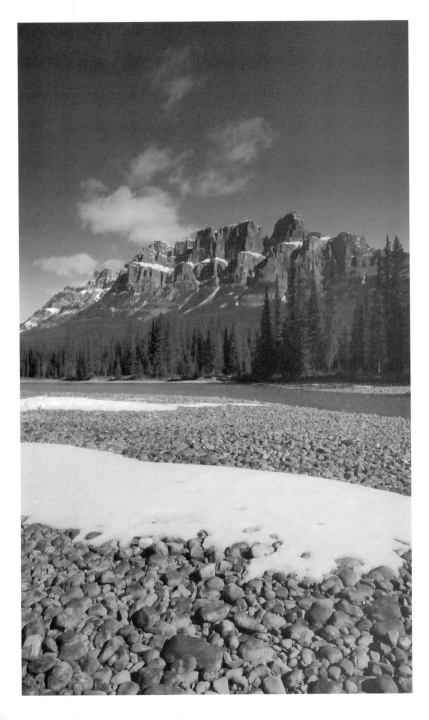

# Overview of the Nikon D50

## Design

The Nikon D50 is designed to not only meet the needs of beginning digital SLR (single-lens-reflex) owners "straight-out-of-the box," but to also give more experienced digital photographers the ability to control the camera on any level they desire. The D50 has benefited from the rapid advances in digital imaging and externally appears very similar to its, recently introduced, more expensive stablemate—the D70s. The camera has even inherited a modified version of the exposure and flash metering system from Nikon's professional D2-series of digital SLR cameras.

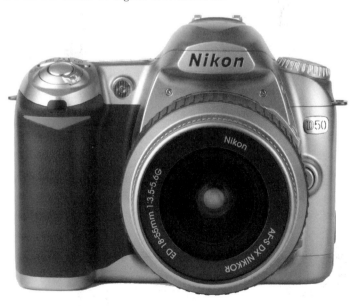

*The D50's Landscape Vari-Program is designed to use a smaller aperture to maximize depth of field. By focusing about 1/3 of the way into the composition you can maximize sharpness throughout the scene for stunning results such as this.*

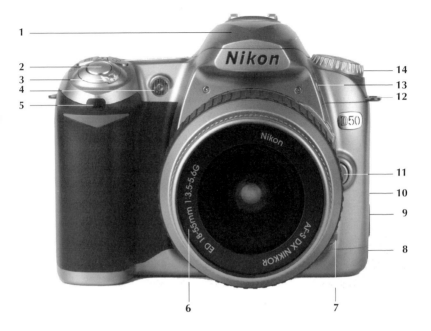

## Front View

1. *Prism/cover for built-in Speedlight*

2. *Shutter release button*

3. *Power switch*

4. *AF-assist illuminator, self-timer/red-eye reduction lamp*

5. *Infrared receiver*

6. *Lens*

7. *Focus mode selector switch*

8. *DC-in connector (under cover)*

9. *Video connector (under cover)*

10. *USB connector (under cover)*

11. *Lens release button*

12. *Strap eyelet*

13. *❹ Flash sync/exposure compensation button*

14. *Mode dial*

18

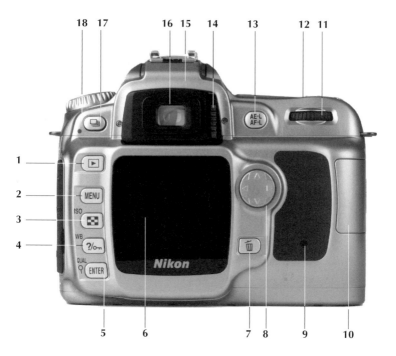

## Back View

1.  ▶ Playback button
2.  MENU Menu button
3.  ☒ Thumbnail button
4.  ?⟋⟍ Help/protect button
5.  ENTER Enter button
6.  LCD monitor
7.  ◗ Delete button
8.  ⟨◌⟩ Multi-selector switch
9.  Memory card access lamp

10. Cover for memory card slot
11. Command dial
12. Control panel
13. ◉ AE/AF lock button
14. Diopter adjustment control
15. Eyecup
16. Viewfinder
17. ◉ Shooting mode button
18. Reset button

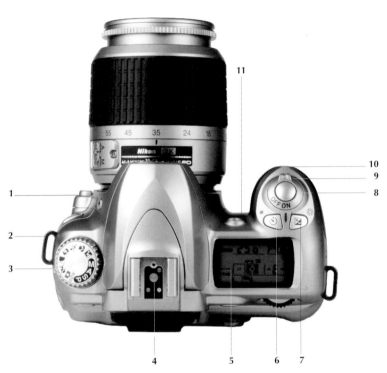

## Top View

1. Lens release button
2. Strap eyelet
3. Mode dial
4. Hot shoe
5. Control panel
6. ⟳ Self-timer/remote control button

7. ⊠ Exposure compensation button
8. Shutter release
9. Power switch
10. Infrared receiver
11. AF-assist illuminator, self-timer/red-eye reduction lamp

The D50 is an interchangeable lens, digital SLR camera that offers complete automation of exposure and focusing, as well as full manual control of all its features and functions. The camera body is 5.2 x 4.0 x 3.0 inches (133 x 102 x 76 mm) and weighs approximately 19 ounces (540 g) without battery or memory card. It has a Nikon F lens mount with autofocus (AF) coupling and contacts; the greatest level of compatibility is achieved with either Nikkor AF-D, or AF-G type lenses. Other CPU and non-CPU Nikkor lens can be used but provide a variable level of compatibility dependent on the type of lens. Data storage is to a Secure Digital (SD) memory card.

## Power

A single EN-EL3 (7.4V 1400mAh) rechargeable lithium-ion battery that weighs approximately 2.8 oz (80 g) powers the D50. Battery performance is dependent on a number of factors, including condition of the battery, the camera functions used and the ambient temperature. At a normal room temperature of 68°F (20°C) it is quite possible to make many hundreds of exposures on a single fully charged EN-EL3. The Nikon EH-5 AC adapter can also be used to power the D50 for extended periods of use.

**Hint:** All electronically controlled cameras very occasionally exhibit some strange behavior with unexpected icons or characters appearing in the LCD display, or the camera ceases to function properly. This is usually due to an electrostatic charge. To remedy the situation try switching the camera off, removing and replacing the battery, or disconnecting then reconnecting the AC power supply, then switching the camera on again. If the problem persists, push the reset button located toward the left end of the camera's baseplate.

## Sensor

The Charge Coupled Device (CCD) sensor used in the D50 is identical to the one used in the D70/D70s, and it is unique to these camera models. It has a total of 6.24 million pixels, of which 3008 x 2000 are image forming, giving the camera a maximum effective resolution of 6.1Mp. Each pixel site is 7 microns square, much larger than those on the sensors of the Nikon Coolpix range, which is why the D50 will generally produce a far superior image to smaller consumer digital cameras.

The imaging area is 0.66 x 1 inches (15.6 x 23.7mm), which is smaller than a 35mm film frame of 1 x 1.5 inches (24 x 36mm) but retains the same 2:3 aspect ratio. Nikon refers to this as its DX-format and uses this designation to identify those lenses that can only be used on its digital SLR cameras. Due to the smaller size of the digital sensor, the focal length of a 35mm film format lens should be multiplied by 1.5x to visualize its view captured by the sensor, although to be strictly accurate the factor is nearer to 1.52x.

In front of the CCD sensor is a filter array, which has four specific purposes:

**Bayer Pattern Filter**
The pixel sites on the CCD do not see in color. They only detect a level of brightness. To impart color to the image, a series of minute red, green, and blue filters are arranged over it in a Bayer pattern, named after the Kodak engineer who invented it. These filters are arranged in an alternating pattern of red/green on the odd-numbered rows, and green/blue on the even-numbered rows. The final image, which is comprised of 50% green, 25% red, and 25% blue, is reconstructed by interpolating the values at each pixel site.

**Micro-Lens Layer**
A CCD sensor is most efficient when the light striking it is perpendicular to its surface. A filter array consisting of a layer of micro-lenses helps realign the light rays projected by the camera lens with the pixel sites on the sensor.

22

**Low Pass Anti-Aliasing Filter**

When you take a picture of a scene that contains very fine detail (e.g. the weave pattern in a piece of material), it is possible that the frequency of this detail is close to that of the pixel sites on the sensor. This can lead to color fringes appearing between two areas of different color or tone on either side of a distinct edge. The low pass filter lowers the acuity of, or softens, the image formed on the sensor to reduce the risk of this occurring.

**Infrared Filter**

Although not visible to the human eye, infrared (IR) light is detected by a CCD sensor. This is a problem because IR light can cause a perceived loss of image sharpness, reduced contrast, and other unwanted effects. Therefore, a filter is incorporated into the filter array to remove most but not all IR light.

# File Formats

The D50 creates two types of files: files compressed using the JPEG (Joint Photographic Experts Group) standard; and files compressed in Nikon's proprietary RAW Nikon Electronic File (NEF) format.

The files using the JPEG standard can be saved at three different sizes, Fine (low compression 1:4), Normal (medium compression 1:8), and Low (high compression 1:16).

*Note:* As the level of compression is increased there is a greater loss of detail in the image. Furthermore, all JPEG compressed files are saved to an 8-bit format, which reduces the tonal range of the image.

The highest quality results come from the NEF format files, as these contain the compressed data direct from the sensor, with virtually no interpolation or camera processing. Nikon claims that the compression of the 12-bit NEF files is lossless, but in truth it is not. The in-camera compression averages out the highlight data to reduce the file size, and when this is converted back to a 12-bit form, highlight tones are restricted. However, since the human eye is unlikely to resolve this change, it would be fair to describe the system a visually lossless. To get the most out of NEF files you will need additional software such as Nikon Capture.

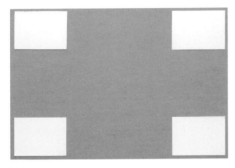

*The narrow border around the outside of the rectangle is the portion of the frame area that you do not see in the viewfinder.*

## The Viewfinder

The D50's eyelevel finder is comprised of a fixed, optical pentaprism, which shows approximately 95% (vertical and horizontal) of the full frame. It has an eyepoint of 18mm (-1.0m$^{-1}$), which is reasonably good for users who wear eyeglasses, plus there is a built-in diopter adjustment between 1.6 to +0.5m$^{-1}$. To set the diopter, mount a lens on the camera and focus it at infinity. Point the camera at a plain surface that fills the frame. Shift the sliding button to the right of the viewfinder eyepiece up or down until the viewfinder's AF brackets appear sharp. It is essential to do this to ensure you see the sharpest view of the focusing screen. Since the built-in correction is not particularly strong, optional eyepiece correction lenses are available between 5 to +3m$^{-1}$.

*Note:* The supplied DK-20 rubber eyecup must be removed to fit optional correction lenses.

The focusing screen is fixed and the viewfinder provides a magnification of approximately 0.75x. The viewfinder display includes essential information about exposure and focus, including focus confirmation, shutter speed, lens aperture, battery sta-

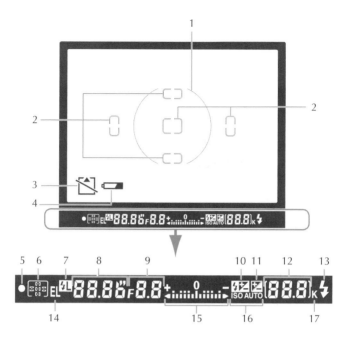

## Viewfinder Display

1. 8mm (0.31") reference circle for center-weighted metering
2. Focus brackets (focus areas)/Spot metering targets
3. No memory card alert
4. Battery status
5. Focus indicator
6. Focus area/AF-area mode
7. Autoexposure (AE) lock/FV lock indicator
8. Shutter speed
9. Aperture (f/number)
10. Flash compensation indicator
11. Exposure compensation indicator

12. Number of exposures remaining/Number of shots remaining before memory buffer fills/Preset white balance recording indicator/Exposure compensation value/Flash compensation value/PC mode indicator
13. Flash-ready indicator
14. AE Lock
15. Electronic analog exposure display/Exposure compensation
16. Auto sensitivity indicator
17. "K" (appears when memory remains for over 1000 exposures)

tus, and flash ready signal. The screen is marked with a central 8mm reference circle for the center-weighted metering, five focus brackets (AF area/spot meter reference zones), and warning symbols to indicate that no memory card is inserted in the camera, and the status of the battery (see Viewfinder Display page 25). The D50 is supplied with the DK-20 eyepiece cap, used to prevent light from entering the viewfinder eyepiece when the camera is not against the photographer's eye.

## Autofocus

The autofocus system is based on the CAM900 AF module used in the Nikon D70s digital SLR camera. It features five sensors arranged in a cross array. The central sensor is a cross type, whereas the other four (top, bottom, left, and right) are single-line sensors. This makes focusing on subjects at the center of the frame fast and positive. However, there can be a tendency for the AF system to "hunt" when using the outer four sensors with certain subjects, particularly in low light.

The detection range of the AF system is –1 to +19EV, which Nikon curiously specifies at an ISO 100 although the camera's base sensitivity is ISO 200! For low light levels there is an AF assist lamp, which has an effective range from 1 foot, 8 inches to 9 feet, 10 inches (0.5 to 3m). The system has three focusing modes AF-A (the default setting that provides automatic selection of either AF-S, or AF-C), AF-S (Single-servo AF), and AF-C (Continuous-servo AF). There are three AF-area modes, Single-area AF, Dynamic-area AF, and Dynamic area AF with Closest Subject Priority. The camera will automatically detect if a subject is moving and initiate focus tracking.

## Exposure Modes

The D50 offers a fully automatic AUTO exposure mode, which does not allow any adjustments by the user. There are an additional six automatic modes that Nikon refers to as Digital Vari-Program modes: Portrait, Landscape, Child,

Sports, Close-up, and Night Portrait. In addition, four user controlled exposure modes are also available: Auto Multi Program (P); Aperture-Priority Auto (A); Shutter-Priority Auto (S); and Manual (M). It is this choice of exposure modes that is the basis of the ability of the D50 to be used as either a simple point-and-shoot camera or a fully-fledged tool for creative photography.

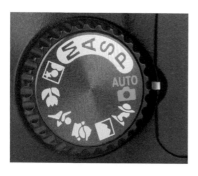

*Use the Mode dial to select from an array of exposure modes that allow you to capture excellent photos in all types of shooting conditions.*

## Exposure Control

The D50 offers three light metering options to cope with a variety of different lighting situations:

### 3D Color Matrix Metering
A 420 pixel RGB sensor within the camera's viewfinder controls this metering method. With either a D-type or G-type Nikkor lens mounted, the system takes into account information about the focused distance, which helps the camera determine where the main subject is located in the frame.

*Note:* Standard Color Matrix metering is activated if other CPU lenses are mounted.

### Center-Weighted Metering
The camera meters the entire area of the frame, but assigns a bias to a central 0.31 inch (8mm) diameter circle (as marked on the focusing screen) in a ratio of 75:25.

**Spot Metering**

The camera meters a 0.12 inch (3.5mm) circle centered on the selected (active) focus area brackets.

The 3D Matrix and center-weighted metering systems have an exposure value (EV) range of 0 to 20EV, and 2 to 20EV for spot metering (ISO 100).

Exposure compensation can be set over a range of –5 to +5 stops in increments of 1/3 or 1/2EV, and exposure and/or flash exposure bracketing is available over +/-2 stops using 3 frame sequences in increments of 1/3 or 1/2EV.

In the user controlled modes that are partially automated (P, S, and A), the exposure settings can be locked with the AE-L/AF-L button located on the rear of the camera to the left of the viewfinder eyepiece.

**Hint:** If you set the D50 to AUTO Mode or one of the six Digital Vari-Program modes, the camera restores the default exposure setting for the selected mode. You surrender all exposure control to the camera, and have no say in the choice of metering system, or use of the flexible program, exposure compensation, bracketing, and flash bracketing functions. However, the Auto-Exposure Lock feature does operate in these modes.

# White Balance

The D50 offers several choices for white balance control. There is a fully automatic option **A** that uses the same 420 pixel RGB sensor in the viewfinder as the metering system. There are also six user-selectable options for specific lighting conditions: Tungsten ☀ for incandescent lighting; Fluorescent ☀ for fluorescent lighting; Direct Sunlight ☀ ; Flash ⚡ for lighting by both internal and external flash units; Cloudy ☁ for daylight under an overcast sky; and Shade 🏠 for daylight in deep shade. Each setting can be fine tuned using the white balance bracketing feature (CS-12).

There is also a Pre-set **PRE** option that can be utilized by taking a reading from a white or gray card under the prevailing lighting conditions.

## Image Processing

In P, S, A, and M modes, image attributes including sharpening, contrast, color mode, saturation, and hue are optimized automatically for a range of pre-set options: Normal, Vivid, Sharper, Softer, Direct Print, Portrait, or Landscape. There is also a Custom option for photographers to define their own values. Nikon calls this system Optimizing Images. Note that when one of the Vari-Program modes is selected, the D50 automatically assigns a set of values according to which mode is active and the photographer has no independent control over this feature.

## The Shutter

The D50 has a combined mechanical and electronic shutter. All shutter speeds up to 1/250 are controlled mechanically; all speeds above this are controlled electronically by opening the shutter for 1/250 second and then switching the sensor on and off to emulate the effect of the shutter opening and closing. This system has a beneficial side effect of allowing a higher flash sync speed of 1/500.

The shutter speed range runs from 30 seconds to 1/4000 and can be set in increments of 1/3 or 1/2EV (CS-11). There is a bulb option for exposures longer than 30 seconds.

## Sensitivity

The D50 allows sensitivity to be set over a range equivalent to ISO ratings of 200 to 1600 in steps of one whole stop (I EV).

**Hint:** To maximize image quality always set the sensitivity (ISO equivalent) to the lowest possible level for the prevailing light conditions.

## Shooting Modes

The shooting mode determines when the camera makes an exposure. In Single Frame the camera takes a single photograph each time the shutter release button is fully depressed. In Continuous mode the camera shutter cycles up to a maximum rate of 2.5 frames per second but this can be limited by a number of factors, including the camera functions that are active, the selected shutter speed, and the remaining capacity of the memory buffer.

### Self-Timer Mode
The camera has a self-timer option with a variable time delay that is set via CS-19; the default is 10 seconds. This feature is useful for self-portraits, or reducing loss of sharpness caused by the effect of camera vibration. The shutter of the D50 can be released remotely using the ML-L3 infrared remote control.

## LCD Monitor

On the rear of the D50 is a 2 inch, 130,000 pixel color LCD monitor, which, unlike the viewfinder, displays 100% of the image file. The brightness of the monitor can be adjusted via the Setup Menu.

Pictures can be reviewed as either a single image or in multiples. By using the multi-selector switch you can scroll through a range of pages containing shooting information, which are superimposed on images reviewed in single-image playback. These include two pages of shooting data, and single pages showing file information, a histogram, or a highlight warning option that causes potentially over exposed areas to flash. You can edit your pictures while they are still

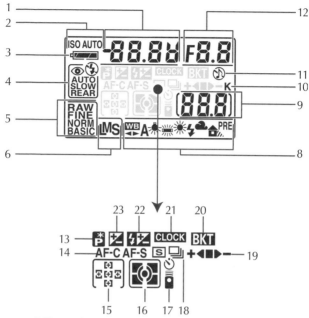

## Control Panel

1. Shutter speed/exposure & flash compensation value/ISO equivalency
2. ISO/AUTO indicator
3. Battery status
4. Flash sync mode
5. Image quality
6. Image size
7. White balance mode
8. No. exposures remaining/no. shots before buffer fills/preset WB/PC mode
9. K indicates memory remains for 1000 exposures
10. Visual beep
11. Aperture/PC mode indicator
12. Flash compensation indicator
13. Exposure compensation indicator
14. Flexible program indicator
15. Focus area/AF-area mode
16. AF mode
17. Metering mode
18. Self-timer/remote control indicator
19. Bracketing progress
20. Bracketing indicator
21. Clock battery status
22. Shooting mode
23. Flash compensation indicator

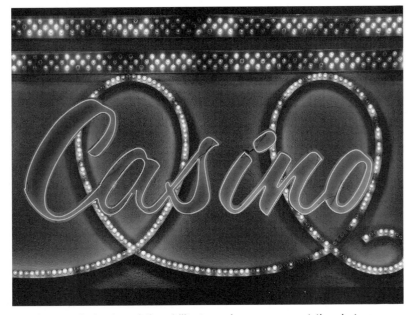

*Image playback and the ability to make sure you got the shot you want, with tricky exposures such as this, is just one of the many benefits of a digital SLR camera.*

held in the camera by reviewing them on the LCD Monitor, with the option to delete them, or protect them from being deleted unintentionally.

In addition to the image playback the LCD Monitor is used to display the various camera menus from where the photographer can activate or deactivate functions and features.

## Menus

Although most of the principle controls of the D50 are easily accessed and operated by buttons or dials located on the camera body there are some core functions that must be set via the camera's four menus: Playback ▶, Shooting ◻, Custom Settings ✐ , and Setup ⚊. To open the menu display you press the Menu button [MENU] on the rear panel of the camera to the right of the LCD Monitor. First select the appropriate menu by using the multi-selector switch. The various options and sub-options are color coded to facilitate navigation and selection of the required setting.

## Control Panel

This small monochrome LCD display on the top plate of the D50 should not be confused with the color LCD Monitor on the rear of the camera. If the D50 is switched OFF, the only information that is visible in the Control Panel is the number of remaining frames available on the installed memory card, and if no card is inserted the display shows "E" to indicate empty. As soon as the camera is powered on, the display shows a range of camera control settings, including battery status, shutter speed, aperture, shooting mode, active focus sensor and focus mode, white balance, audible warning, and image quality and size. Other controls will be indicated as and when they are activated.

## Built-In Speedlight (Flash)

Nikon always refers to their flash units, whether built-in or external, as Speedlights. The D50 has a pop-up Speedlight housed above the viewfinder. In Auto, Portrait, Child, Close-up, and Night-Portrait Modes, the flash will activate automatically if the camera determines the light level is sufficiently low to require additional light. In P, S, A, and M modes, the flash can be activated manually by pressing the Speedlight lock-release button [⚡] on the left side of the viewfinder head. At full output the guide number (GN) of the Speedlight is 49/15 (ft/m, ISO 200) in automatic mode and GN 56/17 (ft/m, ISO 200) in manual mode. It can be used with any CPU lens with a focal length of 20mm to 300mm, and non-CPU (Ai-S, Ai, or Ai modified) lenses with focal lengths of 20 to 200mm.

*Note:* The minimum distance at which the Speedlight can be used is 2 feet (0.6m). However, with certain lenses the minimum distance is greater because the lens may prevent the flash from illuminating the entire subject at close ranges.

The built-in flash is fully compatible with Nikon's latest i-TTL flash exposure control system for balanced fill flash, but defaults to standard i-TTL flash when spot metering or M exposure mode is selected. The D50 is also compatible with the Nikon SB-800 and SB-600 Speedlights, including their Advanced Wireless Lighting control.

## External Ports

On the left of the D50 are ports for connecting accessories. The lower outlet accepts the EH-5 AC adapter and the middle accepts a video cable for connecting the camera to a TV set for image playback. The outlet at the top is a port for connecting the camera to a computer or other data storage device. The camera supports High-speed USB (2.0) with a maximum data transfer rate of 480 Mbps.

# Nikon Lens Limitations with the Built-in Flash

| Lens | Zoom position | Minimum Range |
|------|---------------|---------------|
| AF–S DX ED 12–24mm f/4G | 20mm<br>24mm | 2.5m/8'2"<br>1.0m/33" |
| AF–S ED 17–35mm f/2.8D | 20 mm, 24mm<br>28mm<br>35mm | 2.5m/8'2"<br>1.0m/3'3"<br>0.6m/2' |
| AF–S DX IF ED 17–55mm f/2.8G | 20mm, 24mm<br>28mm<br>35mm<br>45–55mm | 2.5m/8'2"<br>1.5m/4'II"<br>0.7m/2'4"<br>0.6m/2' |
| AF ED 18–35mm f/3.5–4.5D | 18mm, 21 mm<br>24mm<br>28–35 mm | 2.0 m/6'7"<br>0.7m/2'4"<br>0.6m/2' |
| AF 2O–35mm f/2.8D | 20mm<br>24mm<br>28–35mm | 1.5m/4'1 1<br>1.0m/3'3"<br>0.6m/2' |
| AF–S VR ED 24–120mm f/3.5–5.6G | 24mm<br>28–120mm | 0.8m/2'7"<br>0.6m/2' |
| AF–S ED 28–70 mm f/2.8D | 28mm<br>35mm<br>50–70mm | 3.0m/9'10"<br>1.0m/3'3"<br>0.6m/2' |
| AF–S VR 200–400 mm f/4G | 200mm<br>250mm<br>300–400mm | 4.0m/13'I"<br>2.5 m/8'2"<br>0.6m/2' |
| AF–S 18–70 mm f/3.5–4.SG | 18mm<br>24–70mm | 1.0m/3'3"<br>0.6m/2' |

35

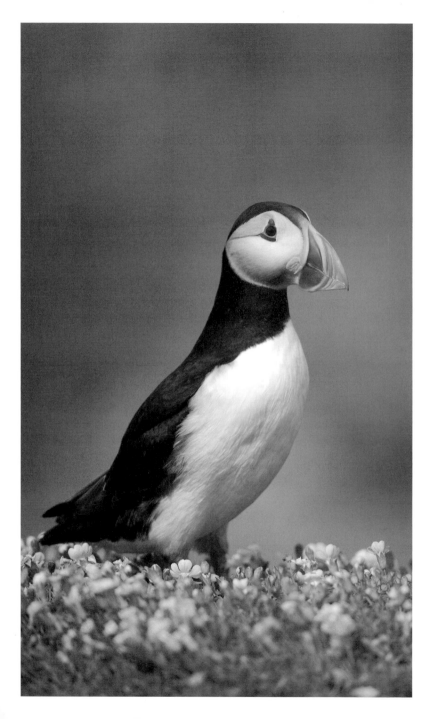

# Quick Start-Up Guide

If you are like most new camera owners you are eager to take some pictures. However, first, there are a few basic steps that you need to take to prepare the camera. It is also well worth spending a little time to acquaint yourself with the principal controls and functions.

## Attaching the Camera Strap

For camera safety, it is essential to first attach the camera strap because it helps prevent the camera from being dropped accidentally and keeps it positioned for fast picture taking. Thread one end of the strap from the outside through the left strap lug and feed it through the keeper-loop. Then pass it through the inside of the buckle under the section of the strap that already passes through the buckle, before pulling it tight. Adjust the length, and then thread the other end through the right strap lug and repeat as described above.

## Inserting the Battery

The D50 is entirely dependent on electrical power, so at the risk of stating the obvious, it is crucial that the EN-EL3/EN-EL3a battery is fully charged. There is no need to pre-condition the battery, but for its first charge, leave it connected to the MH-18a charger until it is cool to the touch. Do not be tempted to remove it as soon as the charge indicator lamp on the MH-18a has stopped flashing.

*The D50 uses a Secure Digital (SD) memory card, which should always be formatted in the camera before its initial use and after downloading pictures. Once it is formatted and inserted in the camera, the card is ready to accept image files. The number of exposures remaining will be indicated in the camera's Control Panel.*

*Make sure the bat-
tery charge cycle is
completely finished
by allowing the bat-
tery to cool in the
charger before you
remove it to insert
into the camera.*

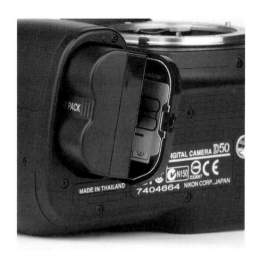

Make sure the camera power switch is set to OFF. Turn the camera over and slide the battery-chamber cover lock toward the center of the camera. Open the cover and insert the battery, making sure its two contacts face the battery-chamber cover and enter first. Lower the battery into place and then press the chamber cover down until it locks; you should hear it click into place. Now turn the camera power switch to ON, and check the battery-status indicator in the upper-left corner of the Control Panel on the camera's right top.

**Choosing a Language**

The first time the D50 is switched ON, the language selection dialog box, from the Setup menu, will appear in the LCD monitor, and the CLOCK icon will flash in the Control Panel. Scroll through the list of languages by pressing the up and down arrows on the multi-selector switch. Once the desired language is highlighted, press the right arrow on the multi-selector switch to select it.

*Note:* OK is displayed next to the name of the highlighted language.

## Setting the Internal Clock

The D50 has an internal clock powered by a built-in rechargeable battery, which is automatically recharged with power from the camera's battery or AC supply.

*Note:* This battery is not accessible by the user.

Once you have selected a language, the Date menu from the Setup Menu will be displayed in the LCD Monitor. The *Year* will be highlighted in yellow (default is 2005). To change it, use the up and down arrows on the multi-selector switch to select the year and move the cursor to the next box to set the month, press the arrow. To confirm language and calendar/clock settings, press the 🔲 button. This also turns the monitor off.

**Hint:** Unless you complete the language and calendar/clock set-up as described above, the shutter release will be inoperative and no other camera functions can be performed.

**Hint:** The internal clock is not as accurate as most wristwatches and domestic clocks. So it is important to check it regularly.

## Mounting a Lens

To take advantage of all the functions and features of the D50, you must use either a G- or D-type Nikkor lens (see page 189 for more details).

It is important to turn off the camera whenever you mount or remove a lens. Identify the mounting index mark on the lens and align it with the mounting index-mark next to the camera's bayonet mount. Insert the lens into the camera and rotate the lens counter-clockwise until it locks into place with a positive click.

G-type lenses lack a conventional aperture ring. However, for other types of Nikkor lenses with a CPU, it is necessary to set and lock the lens' aperture ring to its minimum aperture value (highest f/number).

*To mount a lens, align the white index marks and gently insert the lens into the camera body. Rotate the lens counter-clockwise until it click-locks in place.*

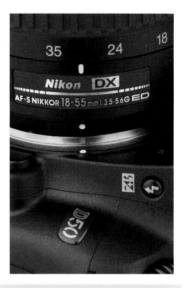

**Hint:** If you turn ON the camera after mounting a lens and flashing *FE E* appears in the Control Panel and viewfinder, the lens has not been set to its minimum aperture value. In this state the shutter release is disabled and the camera will not operate.

## Holding the Camera

Whenever you take pictures with a hand-held camera, it is essential to practice good camera technique to reduce the risk of pictures being blurred due to camera shake. Regardless of whether you want to take a horizontal or vertical shot, the camera should be held with a firm but not overly tight grip. Hold the handgrip in your right hand with your right index finger resting lightly on the shutter release button. Cup your left hand under the camera so that your left index finger and thumb can rotate the zoom/focus ring of the lens. Keep you elbows tucked in towards your body, and stand with your feet shoulder-width apart.

## The Memory Card

The D50 accepts a Secure Digital (SD) memory card for storing images.

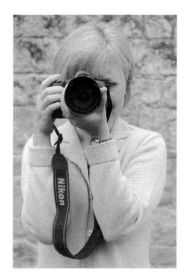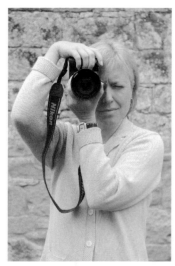

*Practicing good handholding technique is the best way to eliminate results that are less than perfect due to camera shake.*

**Inserting the Memory Card:** First, make sure the camera is switched OFF. Open the card port door by pushing it in the direction (rearward) denoted by the small arrow on its cover. The door will spring open. Insert the card with its contacts pointing toward the camera front facing out. The card will slide in so far and then you will feel a slight resistance. Keep pushing the card so the green memory card access lamp illuminates briefly. Finally, close the card port door. Turn the camera on. If the number of exposures that remain shows in the Control Panel, the card is ready to use. If the format message occurs, then the card needs to be formatted before it can be used.

**Formatting the Memory Card:** All new memory cards must be formatted before first use. To format a card using the D50, insert a card and then switch the camera ON. A message saying, "This card is not formatted. Format card?" will appear in the LCD monitor. Use the multi-selector switch to select "Yes."

*Note:* Because it may damage the memory card, you should never interrupt the power supply to the camera during formatting. Make sure the battery is fully charged before you begin or plug the camera into an AC outlet using the optional EH-5 AC adapter.

During formatting, "FORMATTING" appears in the LCD Monitor. Once formatting is complete, the monitor will shut off and the Contol Panel's frame-count display shows the approximate number of photographs that can be recorded at the current size and quality settings.

**Hint:** Always format the card in the camera—never in a computer. It is good practice to format a card each time you insert it into the camera, even if you have deleted the card's contents using a computer. If you do not do this there is an increased risk of problems occurring with the communication between the memory card and the camera.

*Removing the Memory Card:* To remove a memory card you must make sure that the green memory card access lamp has gone out before switching the camera OFF. Open the card port door and press the card in towards the camera to release it. The memory card will be partially ejected, and can then be pulled out by hand.

If the D50 has no memory card inserted when it is turned on, [-E-] appears in the exposure count brackets.

## Camera Care
Keeping your camera and lenses in a clean, dry environment is very important. But regardless of how scrupulous you are about doing this, dust and dirt will eventually accumulate on your equipment.

Since prevention is better than cure, always keep body and lens caps in place when not using equipment. Always switch the D50 OFF before attaching or detaching a lens to prevent particles being attracted to the low-pass filter by the electrical charge of the sensor. Remember, gravity is your friend! Whenever you change lenses, get into the habit of holding the camera with the front of the body facing downwards. Do not carry or store your D50 on its back, as particles already inside the camera will settle on the low-pass filter.

It also helps to periodically vacuum the interior of your camera bag. It is amazing how much debris can collect there! Sealing you camera body in a clear plastic bag, which you then keep within your camera case, will add another valuable layer of protection in very dusty or damp conditions. It helps to add some sachets of silica gel since they will absorb moisture from the atmosphere within the bag.

**Hint:** Put together a basic cleaning kit with the following: a soft, 1/2-inch (12mm) sable artist's paint brush for general cleaning, a microfiber lens cloth for cleaning lens elements, a microfiber towel (available from any good outdoor or sporting goods store) for absorbing moisture when working in damp conditions, and the rubber-bulb from a blower brush for use with lenses and the low-pass filter.

Always brush or blow material off equipment before wiping it with a cloth. For lens elements and filters, use a microfiber cloth and wipe surfaces in short strokes, not a sweeping circular motion. Turn the cloth frequently to prevent depositing the dirt you have just removed back on the same surface! For any residue that cannot be removed with a dry cloth, you will need to resort to a lens cleaning fluid suitable for photographic lenses. Apply the fluid to the cloth not directly to the lens as it may seep inside and cause damage. Wipe the residue away and then buff the glass with a dry area of the cloth. The lens cloth should be washed on a regular basis to keep it clean.

*Cleaning the Low-Pass Filter:* Dust and any other material that settles on the low-pass filter in front of the CCD sensor will appear as dark spots in your pictures. The exact nature of their appearance will depend on their size and the lens aperture you use. At very large apertures (f/1.4), it is possible that most very small dust specks will not be visible. However, at small apertures (f/22) they are likely to show up as well defined black spots.

To inspect and/or clean the low-pass filter, the D50 has a mirror lock-up function accessed via the Setup menu. Open the menu and scroll to mirror lock-up, then press the multi-selector switch to choose Yes. Press the shutter release and the mirror will rise and stay in its up-position.

*Note:* The Control Panel display will show a series of dashes that flash, and all other information will disappear.

Keep the camera facing down so any debris falls away from the filter; look up in to the mirror box while shining a flashlight on to the low-pass filter. Remember the photosites on the D50's CCD are just 7.8-microns square (one micron = one thousandth of a millimeter) so your eyes will probably not be able to resolve many of the offending particles.

Nikon expressly recommends that you should have the low-pass filter cleaned by an authorized service center. However, this is often impractical for both logistical and financial reasons! Furthermore, they state that under no circumstances should you touch or wipe the filter.

To clean the low-pass filter yourself, keep the camera facing down, and use the rubber bulb from a blower brush to gently puff air towards the filter. Take care that you do not insert any part of the bulb into the camera. Never use a brush or canned compressed air to clean the filter as these can leave a residue, or damage the filter's surface. Once you have finished cleaning, switch the camera OFF to return the mirror to its down position.

If the blower bulb method fails to remove stubborn material, I recommend having the sensor cleaned professionally. For users with plenty of confidence, sensor swabs are available that can be used to wipe the filter clean. It must be stressed that you do this entirely at your own risk, and it is essential that the camera's battery be fully charged before you attempt this procedure. Preferably, use the EH-5 AC adapter to ensure a continuous power supply. If the power supply fails the shutter will close and the mirror will return to its down position, with potentially dire consequences!

Finally, if you have Nikon Capture software you can use the Dust Reference Photo feature of the D50 to remove the effects of dust particles on the low-pass filter by masking their shadow electronically (see page 134), however this is only available for NEF files.

## AUTO—Point and Shoot Photography

The Nikon D50 is designed to operate similarly to 35mm film SLR and has many features in common with other Nikon SLR cameras, both film and digital models. At its simplest level the D50 can be used for straightforward point-and-shoot photography in the fully automatic exposure mode, **AUTO.**

In mode you not only relinquish all exposure control to the camera but you are also locked out of altering several key functions, including autofocus mode, white balance, metering mode, exposure compensation, exposure bracketing, and flash exposure compensation. Nikon has seen fit to include the mode and I am sure a great many D50 owners will use it at least some of the time. Plus, it will be very helpful for other family members and friends for casual shooting. Therefore, this section provides a quick-start guide to using the D50 as a fully automatic camera.

### Mode Dial
Once you have prepared the camera, as described in the previous section, it is ready to take pictures. Rotate the Mode Dial to .

In this mode, camera settings are automatically adjusted to the following values:

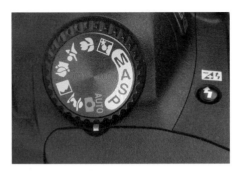

*The mode dial is located on the left top of the camera.*

- **Image Quality:** Normal Pictures are compressed (1:8) using the JPEG standard.

- **Image Size:** Large (L) images are 3,008 x 2,000 pixels in size.

- **Sensitivity:** 200 approximately equivalent to ISO 200

A D- or G-type lens must be mounted for this mode. The camera uses 3D Color Matrix metering and selects single-servo dynamic AF with closest subject priority as the default focus mode. In this mode the shutter can only be released once the camera has acquired sharp focus.

**Check the Camera**

Switch the camera ON. Check that the battery indicator in the control panel shows the battery is fully charged and note the remaining number of available exposures in the frame counter. If the installed memory card has reached it capacity the figure **"FuL 0"** will flash in the frame counter brackets and the shutter speed display will show the word Full. Generally in this state the camera cannot take any more pictures until either one or more pictures is deleted or another memory card is installed. However, it may be possible to take further pictures if you reduce the image quality and size settings.

**Focusing**

Set the focus mode selector switch on the front left of the camera to AF (Autofocus). If you press the shutter release halfway, the camera will focus automatically. However,

*The focus mode selector switch on the lower left front of the camera can be set at either Autofocus (AF) or Manual focus (M).*

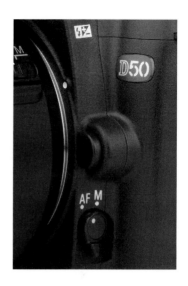

since the 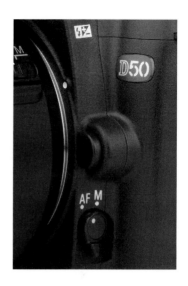 mode sets the AF area mode to closest subject Priority, the camera will automatically select the focus area containing the subject closest to the camera. Once the camera has acquired focus, the audible warning will beep, the active focus area will be highlighted, and the in-focus indicator (●) will appear in the Viewfinder. If the camera is unable to achieve focus, the in-focus indicator will flash, and the shutter release will be disabled (see page 92 for more information).

**Hint:** Remember the D50 shows approximately 95% of the full image frame in its viewfinder. There is a narrow border around all four sides of the viewfinder image that you cannot see but this area will appear in the final picture.

**Exposure**

In 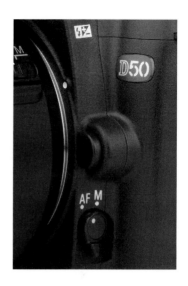 mode, the D50 automatically selects a shutter speed and aperture as soon as you depress the shutter release halfway. Check these chosen values, which are displayed in the viewfinder. If the camera's meter determines that, under the conditions, the picture would be overexposed, ᴴ ᵢ will be displayed. In this case your only option is to attach a neutral density (ND) filter to the front of the lens. If the picture will be underexposed, the camera's built-in Speedlight flash unit will activate automatically. Provided the batteries are in a good state of charge, the flash ready indicator ⚡ will appear in the viewfinder within a couple of seconds. The camera automatically selects an appropriate shutter speed between 1/60th and 1/500th second and sets the flash for Auto front-curtain sync. Alternatively, you can select Auto with red-eye reduction, or flash-off. Other flash modes are not available.

*Note:* The shutter release is disabled until the flash is fully charged and ⚡ is displayed.

To make an exposure squeeze the shutter release button down gently; to prevent camera shake avoid stabbing it with your finger.

*Note:* You can select an alternative focus area mode via Custom Setting 3, but any changes made are only retained while the camera is set to the current mode.

**Hint:** It is important to make sure your subject is within the shooting range of the flash. The built-in Speedlight has a guide number (GN) of 49/15 (ft/m, ISO 200), which means that at an aperture of f/4, and the base sensitivity (equivalent to ISO 200) of the D50, the maximum effective range of the flash unit is 13 feet (4m). If the (insert Blitz icon) flash symbol in the viewfinder blinks after the flash has fired, the shot may be underexposed. In this case, either set a higher sensitivity or move closer to the subject.

**Hint:** To conserve battery power always return the built-in Speedlight to its closed position if it is not in use, otherwise it will continue to draw power so that it remains in a charged and ready state.

## Digital Vari-Program (DVP) Modes

In these DVP modes the D50 uses 3D Color Matrix metering with D or G-type Nikkor lenses, and sets the AF mode to Automatic AF (AF-A), so the user has no control over whether the camera selects single-servo AF mode or continuous-servo AF mode. The AF area mode is set to dynamic AF with closest subject priority as the default except in the Sports and Close-up programs (see below).

**Hint:** The Digital Vari-Programs require a lens with a CPU to be fitted to the D50. If you attach a non-CPU lens the shutter release will be disabled (see page 189 for more details).

**Portrait**

The Portrait mode is designed to select a wide aperture in order to produce a picture with a shallow depth of field. This is desirable for most portraits because it renders the background out of focus so that it does not distract the viewer from the subject. However, the effect is partially dependent on the distance between the subject and the background. This mode is most effective with telephoto or telephoto zoom lenses, and when the subject is relatively far away from the background.

**Hint:** In shooting portraits, the best results are often achieved when the subject fills most of the frame. It is essential that the eyes are in sharp focus, so be sure the active focus area covers at least one of the subject's eyes.

In this mode the D50 uses 3D Matrix metering with D- or G-type lenses, and selects Single-servo Dynamic AF with Closest Subject Priority as the default focus mode. Thus, the shutter can only be released once the camera has acquired sharp focus.

*Note:* You can select an alternative focus area mode via Custom Setting 3, but any changes made are only retained while the camera is set to the current mode.

The built-in Speedlight will be automatically activated in backlit or low-light situations. The camera automatically selects an appropriate shutter speed between 1/60th and 1/500th second and sets the flash for Auto Front-Curtain Sync. Alternatively, you can select Auto with Red-eye Reduction, or Flash-off. Other flash modes are not available.

 ## Landscape

The Landscape Mode is designed to select a small aperture in order to produce a picture with an extended depth-of-field. Generally, this renders everything from the foreground to the horizon in focus, although this will depend on the composition and how close the lens is to the nearest subject. This mode is most effective with wide-angle or wide-angle zoom lenses, and when the scene is well lit.

**Hint:** When using wide-angle focal lengths, try to include some element of interest in the foreground of the scene as well as the middle and far distances.

In this mode the D50 uses 3D Color Matrix metering with D- or G-type lenses, and selects single-servo dynamic AF with closest subject priority as the default focus mode. Thus, the shutter can only be released once the camera has acquired sharp focus.

*Note:* You can select an alternative focus area mode via Custom Setting 3, but any changes made are only retained while the camera is set to Landscape mode.

*Note:* Flash will not activate in the Landscape Mode. The built-in Speedlight and AF-assist lamp are turned off.

 ## Child

The Child Mode is designed to select a wide aperture in order to produce a picture with a shallow depth of field. A de-focused background is preferable in most portrait-photography so that it does not distract the viewer from the subject. However, the effect is partially dependent on the distance between the subject and the background. This mode is most effective with telephoto or telephoto zoom lenses, and when the subject is relatively far away from the background. At the same time the image processing in camera will ensure the color of clothing and backgrounds is rendered vividly while also creating greater subtlety in skin tones.

**Hint:** In shooting portraits, the best results are often achieved when the subject fills most of the frame. It is essential that at least one of the subject's eyes be in sharp focus, so be sure to position the active focus area accordingly when you acquire focus.

**Hint:** Always consider your shooting position when photographing children: A moderate telephoto focal length will allow you to distance yourself a bit from your subjects, reducing the risk of distracting them and thus, allowing you to capture some candid moments. Also, it is often preferable to lower the camera to your subject's eye-level to achieve a more natural and pleasing perspective.

In this mode the D50 uses 3D Matrix metering with D or G-type lenses, and selects single-servo dynamic AF with closest subject priority as the default focus mode. Thus, the shutter can only be released once the camera has acquired sharp focus.

*Note:* You can select an alternative focus area mode via Custom Setting 3, but any changes made are only retained while the camera is set to the current mode.

The built-in Speedlight will be automatically activated in backlit or low-light situations. The camera automatically selects an appropriate shutter speed between 1/60th and 1/500th second and sets the flash for Auto front-curtain sync. Alternatively, you can select Auto with red-eye reduction, or flash-off. Other flash modes are not available.

## Close-Up

The Close-up Mode is designed to select a small aperture in order to produce a picture with an extended depth-of-field for subjects such as flowers, insects, and other small objects. Generally, when working at very short focus distances depth of field is very limited even at small apertures, so this program endeavors to render as much of the subject in focus as possible. To some degree the final effect is dependent on how close the lens is to the subject, because depth of field will be reduced at shorter focus distances. This mode is most effective with lenses that have a close-focusing feature, or dedicated Micro-Nikkor close-up lenses.

**Hint:** Due to the emphasis this mode places on using a small aperture, the shutter speed can quite often be relatively slow. To prevent pictures being spoiled by camera shake, use a tripod in conjunction with either the self-timer function, or ML-L3 Remote Release.

In this mode the D50 uses 3D Color Matrix metering with D- or G-type lenses. Single-servo Single-area AF is the default focus mode, which means the shutter can only be released once the camera has acquired sharp focus.

*Note:* You can select an alternative focus area mode via Custom Setting 3, but any changes made are only retained while the camera is set to the Close-Up mode.

The built-in Speedlight will be turned on automatically in backlit or low-light situations. The camera automatically selects an appropriate shutter speed between 1/125th and 1/500th second and sets the flash for Auto Front-Curtain Sync. Alternatively, you can select Auto with Red-eye Reduction, or Flash-off. Other flash modes are not available.

## Sports

The Sports Mode is designed to select a wider aperture in order to maintain the highest possible shutter speed to freeze motion for fast-paced sports photography or for every-day action such as lively children. It also has a beneficial side effect as this combination produces a picture with a very shallow depth of field that helps to isolate the subject from the background. This mode is most effective with tele-photo or telephoto zoom lenses, and when there are no obstructions between the camera and the subject that may cause the Closest Priority function to focus on something other than the subject.

In this mode the D50's autofocus system will automati-cally track a moving subject and attempt to predict where it will be for each shot, provided you keep the shutter release pressed halfway. The active focus area will be highlighted in the viewfinder, but if the subject moves out of this sensor's coverage, the focus will shift to the next AF sensor area. This makes it possible to follow the action and shoot a sequence of pictures as it occurs.

**Hint:** The D50 has a shutter lag of about 100ms, that is to say that there is a slight but perceptible delay between press-ing the shutter release button and the shutter opening. Therefore, it is important to anticipate the peak moment of the action to record it. If you see it in the viewfinder you will have missed the shot!

In this mode the D50 uses 3D Color Matrix metering with D- or G-type lenses, and selects the center AF sensor (you can change to another using the multi-selector switch). It sets continuous-servo dynamic AF with closest subject prior-ity as the default focus mode, which means the shutter can be released even if the camera has not acquired sharp focus.

*Note:* You can select Single-servo AF via Custom Setting 2, and an alternative focus mode via Custom Setting 3, but these changes are only retained while the camera is set to the Sports mode.

*Note:* There are no flash modes available in the Sports Mode. The built-in Speedlight and AF-assist lamp are turned off.

## Night Portrait

The Night Portrait Mode is designed to capture properly exposed pictures of people against a background that is dimly lit. It is most effective when the background is in low light as opposed to near dark conditions. For example a city scene lit by artificial lighting, or a landscape at twilight. For a foreground subject that is in particularly low light, the built-in Speedlight or an external Speedlight such as the SB-600 can be used to supplement the ambient light.

**Hint:** In this mode the camera may select a long shutter-speed, so be prepared to use a tripod or some other form of camera support to prevent pictures being spoiled by camera shake. If you do not have a tripod, resting the D50 on a solid surface such as a bench or a wall will be just as effective. To prevent camera shake when releasing the shutter, use either the self-timer function or the ML-L3 remote control.

**Hint:** If the camera indicates a shutter speed of 1 second or longer, switch on the long exposure noise Reduction feature from the Shooting Menu to help reduce the level of electronic noise in the picture.

In this mode the D50 uses 3D Color Matrix metering with D- or G-type lenses, and selects single-servo dynamic AF with closest subject priority as the default focus mode, which means the shutter can only be released once the camera has acquired sharp focus.

*Note:* You can select an alternative focus area mode via Custom Setting 3, but changes will only be retained while the camera is set to the current mode.

The built-in Speedlight will be turned on automatically in backlit or low-light situations. The camera automatically selects an appropriate shutter speed between 1 second and 1/500th second and sets the flash for Auto slow-sync. Alternatively, you can select Auto slow-sync with red-eye reduction, or flash-off. Other flash modes are not available.

***Summary Information: Digital Vari-Program Modes***

The following conditions are common to all Digital Vari-Program modes:

- All photographs are recorded in the sRGB color space

- All shooting modes (single, continuous, remote, and remote-delay) can be used

- If the light levels exceed the sensitivity of the D50 either **H i** (scene too bright), or **L o** (scene too dark) will appear in the viewfinder display and control panel.

The following table lists the values that the D50 applies to optimize images shot in the Digital Vari-Program modes

| Digital Vari-Programs | AUTO | | | | | | |
|---|---|---|---|---|---|---|---|
| White balance | Auto | Auto | Auto | Auto | Auto | Auto | Auto |
| Sharpening | Auto | Auto | Auto | Auto | Auto | Auto | Auto |
| Tone comp. | Auto | Auto | Auto | Auto | Auto | Auto | Normal |
| Color mode | IIIa (sRGB) | Ia (sRGB) | IIIa (sRGB) | Ia (sRGB) | IIIa (sRGB) | IIIa (sRGB) | Ia (sRGB) |
| Saturation | Normal | Normal | Normal | Normal | Normal | Normal | Normal |
| Hue | 0 | 0 | 0 | 0 | 0 | 0 | 0 |

# Image Playback

Without doubt the greatest advantage digital photography has over film photography is that any image stored on the memory card can be played back, together with a variety of information about the picture, on the LCD monitor. You can review your picture immediately, allowing you to not only assess it for aesthetic merit, but also analyze it for technical quality as well.

## Simple Playback

At its default setting, the D50 will automatically display the picture on the LCD Monitor while recording to the memory card. The image will remain on the monitor for 20 seconds, but the duration of the display can be adjusted via Custom Setting 17. If you wish to view the picture again press ▶ .

*Note:* The camera will display the most recent picture. To view other pictures, use the multi-selector switch; pressing it right scrolls through pictures in the order in which they were taken, pressing it left shows them in reverse order.

**Hint:** To conserve power, only view pictures for as long as is necessary. To switch the monitor off and return to the shooting mode, the quickest route is to press the shutter release button lightly. Alternatively, you can press the ▶ button.

## Single-Image Playback

The swiftest way to review a single image is to press the ▶ button. This switches the LCD monitor on to display either the most recently taken or most recently displayed image. If you have used the LCD monitor since taking a picture, the D50 will show the last image that you viewed. However, if you have taken a picture since you last used the playback, the camera will show the most recently taken picture.

*Note:* If no images have been stored on the memory card in the current folder, the following message is displayed on the monitor FOLDER CONTAINS NO IMAGES.

**Hint:** If you have Custom Setting 5 set to ON, the picture automatically appears on the monitor after you make an exposure.

As soon as you have finished reviewing the image, you can either press the ▶ Button, or the Shutter Release halfway to switch the monitor off. Alternatively, you can let the auto power-off feature (set via Custom Setting 17) cancel the monitor display after the pre-set monitor-off time has elapsed.

*Note:* The latter option is not good practice if you expect to review a lot of images, since it will use a significant amount of battery power.

*Image Review:* Once you have an image, or images, stored on the memory card in the camera, you can browse through them by pressing ⊕ on the multi-selector switch. When your selected image is displayed, you can summon the image data by scrolling through a series of five information pages by pressing ⊕ on the multi-selector switch. The pages are displayed in the following order if the multi-selector switch is pushed up repeatedly or reverse order if pushed down repeatedly:

*Page 1:* Folder and file name, image size and quality, frame counter (shown in the top right corner; the first figure is the frame number, the second is the total number of frames currently stored in the folder.)

*Page 2:* Camera, date, time, metering mode, shutter speed, lens aperture, exposure mode (plus any compensation factor), and flash mode (if used).

*Page 3:* Image Optimization setting, ISO, white balance value, image size and quality, sharpening, tone, hue, and saturation.

*Page 4:* Shows HIGHLIGHTS to warn of possible overexposure.

*Page 5:* Shows the HISTOGRAM graph of tone distribution.

**Viewing Multiple Images**
You can display multiple images as small thumbnails by pressing the 🔳 button. If you press this button while you have a single image showing, it will display four images on the LCD screen; press it again and 9 images will appear.

*Note:* The size of the thumbnail changes depending on whether four or nine are shown. If the folder contains fewer than either four or nine images, the thumbnails are still shown at the same size as four per page.

When multiple images are displayed, the currently selected image has a yellow border, and pressing the Multi Selector Switch in any direction shifts selection to another image.

*Note:* You cannot access the information pages when images are displayed as thumbnails, even if only one image is displayed on the LCD monitor.

To display a single image, continue to press the ▦ button until it appears.

## Image Review Zoom Function

The D50 allows you to see a magnified view of the image displayed in the LCD monitor. Start by pressing the the ENTER (Q) button. Then press and hold the the ▦ button, which superimposes a thumbnail of the full frame on the main image. Within the thumbnail image is a smaller frame with red borders and blue corner sections. By pressing the Multi Selector Switch, this frame can be moved around inside the area of the thumbnail. Once you have framed the area of the image you wish to magnify, continue to hold down the ▦ button, and now rotate the Command

*The buttons on the back of the D50 to the left of the LCD Monitor are placed for easy access, allowing you to make multiple settings quickly.*

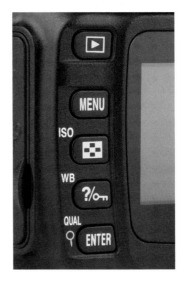

Dial and the size of the red/blue reference frame can be adjusted to select the precise area of the image to be magnified. Finally, release the the 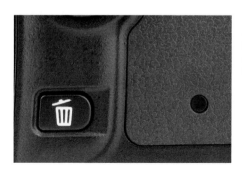 button and the selected area is magnified to fill the LCD monitor screen. If you wish to navigate around the image press the 🔳 button and press the multi-selector switch to move the reference frame. Then release the 🔳 to show the magnified view of the chosen selection.

## Protecting Images

If you want to protect a displayed image from accidental deletion, press the the 🔲 button. A the 🔲 appears in the top left corner of the image to indicate it is protected.

*Note:* Protected files are marked as read-only even when they are transferred to a computer, or other storage device.

To remove protection, simply press the the 🔲 button again, and the 🔲 will disappear.

## Deleting Images

To delete an image, first display it on the LCD Monitor, either as a full frame image or as thumbnail (make sure the thumbnail of the image you wish to delete is highlighted by a yellow border). Then press the the 🗑 button. A Delete? 🔲 Yes message is displayed ⊙ Cancel. Press the button again to confirm and effect the deletion.

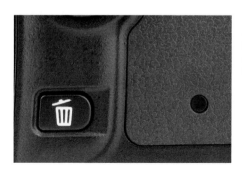

*You must press the Delete button two times to delete an image file from the memory card.*

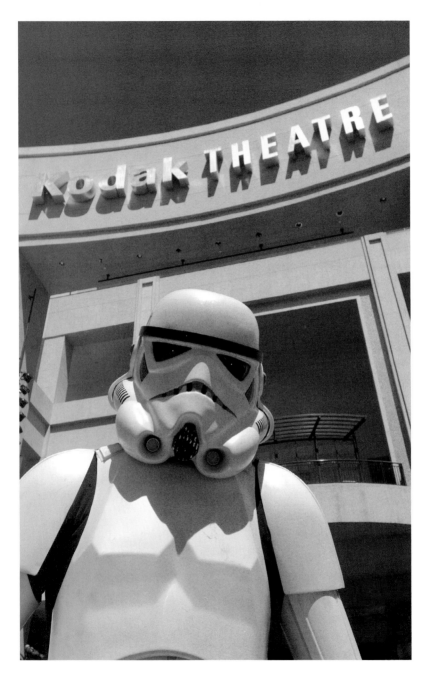

## Automatic Speedlight Function

If the D50 determines that additional lighting is required in
🔲, ⚡, ⚡, ☘, and 🖼 modes, the built-in Speedlight will
pop-up automatically when the Shutter Release is pressed
halfway. Once raised, the D50 will only take a photograph if
the ⚡ flash-ready indicator is displayed in the viewfinder.
If it does not appear, the flash is still charging. Wait until
⚡ appears before pressing the shutter release again.

Flash operation can be cancelled, if you wish, by pressing and holding down the ➊ Flash Sync Mode Button on
the left side of the viewfinder head, and then rotating the
Command Dial until 🚫 appears in the Control Panel.
Alternatively you can use the same method to select 🖼⚡
Auto-flash with Red-eye Reduction to reduce the effect of
light reflecting from the retinas of a subject's eyes.

**Hint:** To conserve battery power always return the Speedlight to its closed position by pressing it down gently when
you no longer require it.

↺ *In Portrait mode the built-in Speedlight flash will pop-up and fire
automatically when it is needed. In this case, the camera determined
that a little extra front fill flash was needed for the best exposure.*

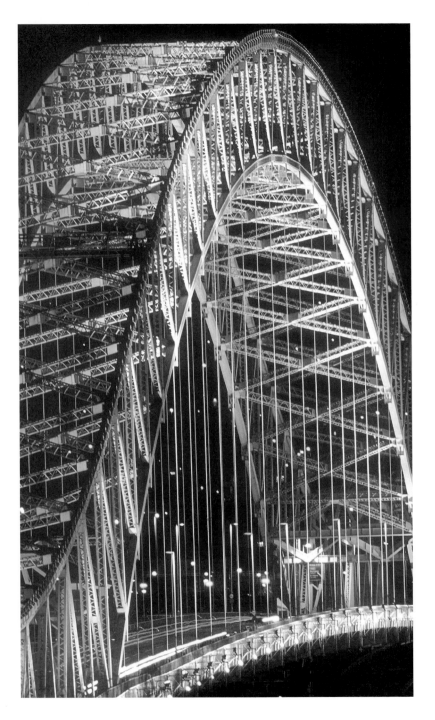

# D50 Shooting Operations in Detail

## Powering the D50

The D50 is powered by an EN-EL3 or EN-EL3a rechargeable Lithium-ion battery, each of which weighs approximately 2.8 oz (80 g). The battery is designed so that it can only be correctly inserted into the camera. It is charged using the dedicated MH-18a Quick Charger (supplied with the camera). A fully discharged battery can be completely recharged in approximately 120 minutes using the MH-18 or MH-18a. Unlike some other types of rechargeable batteries, the EN-EL3/EN-EL3a does not require conditioning prior to first use. However, it is advisable to ensure that the initial charge cycle for a new battery is continued until the battery cools down before removing it from the charger. Do not be tempted to remove it as soon as the indicator lamp on the charger stops flashing.

*Note:* The MH-18 Quick Charger (supplied with the D100 and D70 cameras) and MH-19 Multi-Charger can also be used to charge the EN-EL3; charging times are approximately the same as with the MH-18a.

### Using the Battery
*To insert the battery:*
1. Make sure the power switch is in the OFF position. Invert the camera and push the small button on the battery chamber lid toward the tripod socket. The battery chamber lid should swing open.
2. Open the lid fully and slide the battery into the camera, observing the diagram on the inside of the chamber lid.
3. Press the lid down (you will feel a slight resistance) until it locks (you will hear a slight click as the latch closes).

*Many factors play a part in determining how many shots you will get from a fully charged battery. These include: the use of flash, the LCD monitor, and the vibration reduction feature found on some Nikkor lenses.*

### To remove the battery:

1. Make sure the power switch is in the OFF position. Invert the camera and push the small button on the battery chamber lid toward the tripod socket. The battery chamber lid should swing open.
2. Hold the lid open, turn the camera upright, and allow the battery to slide out taking care that it does not drop.
3. Close the battery chamber lid.

Again, whenever you insert or remove a battery, it is essential that you set the power switch of the D50 to the OFF position. If you make any changes to the camera settings and then remove the battery while the power switch is still set to the ON position, the D50 will not retain the new settings. Likewise, if the camera is still in the process of transferring data from the buffer memory to the storage media when the battery is removed and the power switch is set to ON, image files will be corrupted, or lost.

### To charge the battery:

1. Connect the MH-18a to an AC power supply. (The MH-18a can be used worldwide, connected to any AC outlet, at any voltage from 100V to 250V, via an appropriate socket adapter).
2. Align the slots on the side of the battery with the four lugs (two each side) on the top of the MH-18a and lower the battery before sliding it toward the indicator lamp until it locks in place. The charge lamp should begin to flash immediately, indicating that charging has commenced. A full charge of a completely discharged battery will take approximately 120 minutes.

*The MH-18/MH-18a will recharge a depleted Lithium-ion battery in about two hours.*

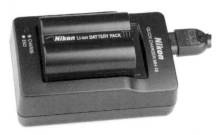

## Battery Tips

- To ensure the battery has recharged fully, do not remove it from the charger as soon as the charge lamp stops flashing. Leave the battery in place until it has cooled to the ambient room temperature.

- Lithium batteries do not exhibit the memory effects associated with NiCd batteries, therefore a partially discharged battery can take a "top-off" charge without adversely affecting battery performance.

- If you carry a spare battery always ensure that you keep the semi-opaque plastic terminal cover in place. Without it there is a risk that the battery terminals may short and cause damage to the battery.

## Alternative Power Sources

*EN-EL3a (7.4V, 1500mAh) rechargeable Lithium-ion battery:*
In addition to the EN-EL3 battery the D50 can be powered by this higher powered version, which according to test results published by the Nikon Corporation will increase shooting capacity by approximately 25%.

*Note:* The EN-EL3 (7.4V, 1400mAh and EN-EL3a (7.4V, 1500mAh) rechargeable Lithium-ion batteries can be charged using any of the following chargers: MH-18, MH-18a, or MH-19. All three chargers can be used worldwide, connected to any AC outlet, at any voltage from 100V to 250V, via an appropriate socket adapter.

## The Clock/Calendar Battery

The D50 has an internal clock/calendar that is powered by a rechargeable battery that is charged automatically by the camera's main power supply. Nikon states that 72 hours of charging is sufficient for about four weeks of clock/calendar backup power. If the CLOCK symbol flashes in the Control Panel, the clock/calendar battery is exhausted and the date/time will have reverted to 2005.01.01 00:00:00. It will need to be reset via the Date option in the Setup menu.

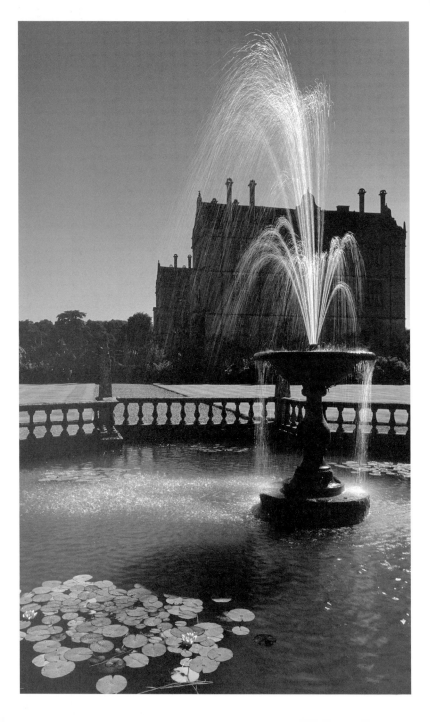

**Note:** Inserting a fully charged battery or powering the camera with an EH-5 AC adapter should recharge the clock/calendar battery. However, if the battery will not hold a charge it will have to be replaced at a Nikon service center. It is not user changeable.

## Battery Performance

Obviously, the more functions the camera has to perform the greater the demand for power. Reducing the number of functions and the duration for which they are active is fundamental to reducing power consumption. Since operation of the D50 is totally dependent on an adequate electrical power supply, the following suggestions tell you how to preserve battery power.

• A fully charged EN-EL3/3a battery, in good condition, will retain its full capacity over a period of a few days. If the battery is unused for a month or more, expect it to suffer a substantial loss of charge, so recharge it fully before use.

• While the autofocus function uses relatively little power, the Vibration Reduction (VR) feature available with some Nikkor lenses reduces battery life by approximately 10% when active.

• Low temperatures cause a change to the internal resistance, which impairs performance of a battery regardless of its type. However, Lithium batteries are fairly resilient in cold conditions. If you are shooting in cold conditions, keep a spare battery in a warm place such as an inside pocket and as the performance of the battery in the camera dwindles, exchange it with the warm one. Allow the used battery time to warm-up again and keep rotating between the two batteries to maximize their shooting capacity.

*Before attempting long exposures, make sure you have a fully charged battery inserted in the camera. It never hurts to have a spare in your camera bag for occasions such as this.*

- Using the D50's color LCD monitor increases power consumption significantly. Unless you need it, turn the monitor OFF. Consider setting CS-5: Image Review to OFF (**Note:** the default setting is ON).

**Hint:** If the Image Review feature is set to ON, as soon as you have checked the picture, press the shutter release button lightly. This prepares the camera to take another picture by immediately switching the LCD Monitor off.

# Image Resolution and Processing

### Image Storage

The D50 stores picture files to Secure Digital (SD) cards; these solid-state cards are capable of retaining data even when they are not powered, and feature a "write-protect" switch to prevent unintentional data loss.

*Note:* If you insert an SD card into the D50 with the write-protect switch set to its 'lock' position it is not possible for the camera to record or delete any photographs, and the card cannot be formatted. (CHA) is displayed in the control panel as a warning.

As SD cards have no moving parts, and use flat plates rather than pins and sockets for electrical contacts they are reasonably robust. Obviously you should treat any card with the same care as you would your camera but a minor knock, or exposure to the natural elements should not cause any problems, although total immersion in water should be avoided! Typically, they have a temperature operating range of –13 F to 185 F (-25C to 85C), and no altitude limit.

### Formatting Memory Cards

The memory of a storage card has a similar structure to that of a hard disk drive, with a file directory, file allocation table, folders, and files. As data is written to and erased from the card, small areas of its memory can become corrupted, which may cause problems the next time you try to access

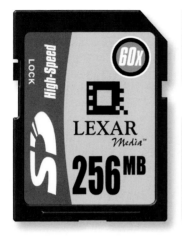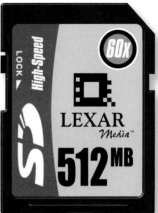

*Secure Digital (SD) cards are available with different storage capacities and feature a "write protect" switch to prevent data loss. Photo © Lexar Media, Inc.*

and/or transfer data held on the card. Therefore, it is good practice to format the SD card each time you insert it in the camera, as this reduces the risk of such problems.

**Note:** Always save you images to a computer or other storage device before formatting a card. Although Nikon state in the D50 instruction book that formatting a memory card "permanently deletes all photographs and any data they contain." this is somewhat misleading. The process of formatting actually causes the existing file directory information to be over-written so that it no longer points to the image data held on the card. It does not erase all the data as Nikon implies. That said, once a card is reformatted it is difficult to recover previously written data from the card.

## Image Format, Quality, and Size

The D50 saves images in two file types: Joint Photographic Experts Group (JPEG) and Nikon Electronic File (NEF). The JPEG uses compression algorithms to reduce the size of the image file by discarding data and then rebuilding the data when the file is opened. This type of compression is known as "lossy." The NEF format used in the D50 also uses compression, so it does not retain the full range of sensor data, but Nikon describes it as being "visually lossless." To eek out every last ounce of quality that the D50 has to offer, shoot in the NEF format!

*Note:* Not all software is capable of reading NEF files. The Nikon Picture Project application supplied with the camera is capable of some basic NEF processing, but the files can only be saved in the JPEG format if you want to export them! Personally I prefer to use either Nikon View 6.2.6, or Nikon Capture 4.3 as they both offer far more flexibility when handling NEF RAW files.

It is important to understand the fundamental difference between the JPEG and NEF format. Images saved in the JPEG standard are processed by the D50 according to the settings either you, or the camera selected at the time of the exposure, whereas NEF format files are subjected to virtually no processing, other than compression, by the camera, and can have many of their attributes adjusted after the event.

As the D50 saves a file as a JPEG, two key things happen to the data:

1) The 12-bit data from the sensor is converted to 8-bit. This will reduce the tonal range of the picture, which can be significant if you intend to perform a lot of processing on an image at a later stage.

2) Camera settings, such as the white balance, sharpening, tone, and hue are assigned to the JPEG by the camera. If, inadvertently, you select the wrong setting, you will need to try and undo your mistake by post processing in a computer, but there is no guarantee this will be successful.

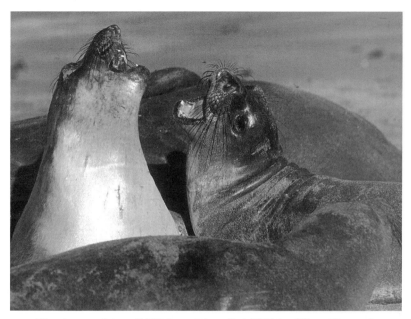

*Nikon's proprietary RAW format is called NEF for Nikon Electronic File. This type of file receives virtually no processing in the camera. NEF files are 12-bit color, which gives a finer rendering of color tones.*

Best results are achieved with the larger file size and finer compression settings, which are ideal if you intend to print your pictures. However, JPEGs are particularly convenient if you want to post pictures to a website or send them as an attachment to email because they can be read by a very wide variety of computer applications, and the format is supported by HTML, the standard computer language used to create web pages. In this case select smaller file size and higher compression.

The D50 allows you to save JPEGs at three sizes:

**L–** Large (3008 x 2000 pixels)
**M–** Medium (2256 x 1496 pixels)
**S–** Small (1504 x 1000 pixels)

For each file size you can assign one of three levels of compression (usually referred to as quality):

**FINE** – uses a low compression of 4:1
**NORMAL** – uses a moderate compression ratio of 8:1
**BASIC** – uses a high compression ratio of 16:1

*Note:* JPEG compression can generate visual artifacts; the higher the compression ratio, the more apparent these become. If you are shooting for web publication this is unlikely to be an issue, but if you intend to make prints from your JPEG file pictures you will probably want to use the Large/FINE settings.

You can configure the D50 to save your images as JPEGs using the Shooting Menu:

Press **MENU** and use the multi-selector switch to open the Shooting menu. Navigate to Image quality and press the ⊙ to open the options page. Scroll down the list, highlight your choice and press the ⊙ to select it.

Stay in the Shooting Menu and select Image Size then press the ⊙ to open the options page. Scroll down the list, highlight your choice and press the ⊙ to select it.

**Hint:** Alternatively, and in my opinion, by far the more convenient and quicker way is to use the button and dial method. Press and hold the **ENTER** button then rotate the command dial to select the image quality/size; as you do this the values will be displayed in the control panel.

*NEF Format:* The NEF format file that Nikon also refers to as a RAW file uses a compressed version of the raw data from the CCD sensor. Nikon describes the compression applied to these files as being "visually lossless," which essentially means that it is impossible to differentiate them from the original data. In fact Nikon uses a partial-compression scheme that only works on certain image data while leaving other data unaffected. Once the analog signal from each pixel site on the D50's CCD sensor has been converted to digital data, it has one of 4096 possible values (described as a 12-bit depth). A value of 0 represents black (there is no data), and a value of 4095 represents pure white. Before the Nikon compression is applied, the camera separates the values that represent the very dark tones from the rest of the data. The data with values that represent the remaining tones is then divided into groups of varying size. The compression is then applied. The values of the very dark tones are not affected, but the multiple values in each group that represent the lighter tones is rounded by the compression process, resulting in the loss of data.

When an application such as Nikon Picture Project or Nikon Capture opens a NEF file it reverses this compression. However, the data discarded by the compression process leaves gaps in the tonal range of the image. Before you panic, let me put this data loss into perspective. Our eye are incapable of resolving the very minor changes that take place (remember Nikon's phrase "virtually lossless"), so the data loss due to the compression process is of no practical consequence.

Shooting NEF format files allows you to make the most of your D50:

- You will get far smoother transitions of tone due to the much wider tonal range of the 12-bit NEF files, compared with the 8-bit JPEG files.

- Image attributes such as sharpening, white balance, tone, and hue are all irreversibly embedded in a JPEG file. Images saved in the NEF format can have these attributes modified in post-capture processing using appropriate software.

To set the D50 to record images in the NEF format follow the instructions given for selecting the JPEG format (see opposite page), but highlight and select the NEF option instead.

*Note:* There is no Image size option with NEF files since the D50 always uses the full 3008 x 2000 pixel resolution of the sensor.

## White Balance

While film has a fixed response to the range of wavelengths of light, the sensor in a digital camera can be adjusted to record specific ranges of wavelengths. This adjustment is known as "white balance."

All sources of light emit a range of different wavelengths, which determines its color. Light that contains primarily short wavelengths, within the visible spectrum, will appear blue (or cool), whereas light that consists mainly of longer wavelengths will appear red (or warm). The color of light is expressed, as color temperature in units of Kelvin, for example many daylight films are balanced to a color temperature of 5400K. However, this is a somewhat arbitrary value since many factors influence the color temperature of daylight, such as time of day and year, altitude, and atmospheric conditions.

Although a color temperature of 5400K is fixed for daylight film, digital cameras sensors can be balanced to a variety of color temperatures. The D50 has eight principal white balance settings:

A **Automatic:** Nikon suggests that the D50 will measure any color temperature between 3500K and 8000K automatically, which is fine if you do not shoot indoors under standard incandescent household lighting that typically has a color temperature of less than 3500K!

 **Incandescent:** Use this indoors in place of Automatic since its color temperature is close to most tungsten based lighting. (3000K)

 **Fluorescent:** This setting is rather a hit and miss affair due to the variability of color and intensity of light emitted from a fluorescent source. (4200K)

 **Direct Sunlight:** For subjects or scenes photographed in direct sunlight during mid-day. At other times, when the sun is lower in the sky, the light is redder, giving a warmer appearance to your pictures. (5400K)

**Flash:** For pictures in which electronic flash is the primary light source. (5200K).

 **Cloudy:** This setting works well when shooting under overcast skies. Typically this type of lighting has a relatively high color temperature imparting a rather cool color cast to subjects. (6000K)

 **Shade:** Is intended for those situations when your subject is in open shade beneath a clear, or nearly clear blue sky. In this instance the lighting will be biased towards blue, as it is comprised principally of light reflected from the blue sky. (8000K)

**PRE** **Preset:** This option allows you to set, manually, a white balance value measured from the lighting on a specific subject or scene. This feature is selected from the Shooting Menu and provides two methods of selecting a white balance value, either from a white or gray card measured by the D50, or by using the white balance value from a previous exposure as a reference. Nikon suggests you can use either a white or gray card as a reference target for the **PRE** option. I suggest you only use a gray card, because a white card is likely to cause exposure problems, unless you are confident about your ability to measure this.

**Hint:** You do not have to follow the white balance settings slavishly according to the prevailing light conditions. You can also use them creatively. For example, if you shoot a sunlit scene with the Shade setting, your picture will have a strong red/yellow cast similar to the effect you would get with a pale amber (Wratten 81C) warming filter. Once again, the great appeal of digital photography is the ability to experiment!

## White Balance Bracketing

In addition to the fixed color temperature values of the white balance settings (all except Automatic) described above, the D50 allows you to fine-tune the white balance by increasing or decreasing these values slightly by using the white balance bracketing feature available via Custom Setting 12. Rather than express the fine-tuning factor in Kelvin, Nikon describes these incremental changes with the rather unhelpful term "Step Value", which can be set to either 1, 2, or, 3, without differentiating between the increase or decrease in color temperature that each setting creates.

After each exposure is made the D50 processes the image data to produce three separate pictures, the first has an unmodified color temperature value ('0' in the table below), the second with slightly warmer (red) colours (minus value in the table below), and the third with slightly cooler (blue) colors (positive value in the table below). The degree of difference between the unmodified color temperature value, and the warmer/cooler versions increase as the value of the Step Value increases.

Approximate color temperature (K) for the Step Values applied during white balance bracketing:

| Step Value | Incandescent | Fluorescent | Direct Sunlight | Flash | Cloudy | Shade |
|---|---|---|---|---|---|---|
| 3 (+) | 2,700K | 2,700K | 4,800K | 4,800K | 5,400K | 6,700K |
| 2 (+) | 2,800K | 3,000K | 4,900K | 5,000K | 5.600K | 7,100K |
| 1 (+) | 2,900K | 3,700K | 5,000K | 5,200K | 5,800K | 7,500K |
| 0 | 3,000K | 4,200K | 5,200K | 5,400K | 6,000K | 8,000K |
| 1 (-) | 3,100K | 5,000K | 5,300K | 5,600K | 6,200K | 8,400K |
| 2 (-) | 3,200K | 6,500K | 5,400K | 5,800K | 6,400K | 8,800K |
| 3 (-) | 3,300K | 7,200K | 5,600K | 6,000K | 6,600K | 9,200K |

*Note:* Because different types of fluorescent lighting can emit a wide band of wavelengths the adjustment increments cover a broader range (from 2,700K to 7,200K) than the other types of lighting.

**Hint:** Even using a Step Value of 3 applies a relatively fine degree of change to the white balance (color temperature), so this feature is probably only worthwhile for critical applications. If you shoot NEF (RAW) files Nikon Capture 4.3 offers a far greater level of control over white balance.

On the D50 the white balance setting can be selected in one of two ways. Press ⬛ and use the multi-selector switch to open the Shooting Menu. Navigate to White Balance and press ◉ to open the options page. Scroll down the list, highlight your choice and press ◉ to select the require value. Alternatively, and by far the quicker way is to use the ⬛ . Press and hold the button, then rotate the command dial to select a white balance setting, as you do this, the value is displayed in the control panel.

**Optimizing Images**

The D50 has several other controls that affect the appearance of your pictures. In the Vari-Program modes these controls are assigned automatically. To make things easier for the user, Nikon has clustered the same controls together in a series of preset options that can be applied to images shot in P, A, S, and M exposure modes. The options available are: Normal, Vivid, Sharper, Softer, Direct Print, Portrait, Landscape, and Custom.

It is important to understand that the Custom option is the only one that allows you to set controls manually. The other seven options all assign controls automatically, with no alternative settings according to the following table:

| | Sharpening | Tone | Color Mode | Saturation | Hue |
|---|---|---|---|---|---|
| **Normal** | Auto | Auto | IIIa | Normal | 0 |
| **Vivid** | Auto | Auto | IIIa | Enhanced | 0 |
| **Sharper** | High | Auto | IIIa | Normal | 0 |
| **Softer** | Low | Auto | IIIa | Normal | 0 |
| **Direct Print** | Medium High | Auto | Ia | Normal | +3 |
| **Portrait** | Medium Low | Auto | Ia | Normal | 0 |
| **Landscape** | Medium High | Auto | IIIa | Normal | 0 |

**Hint:** You will may have noticed that all of the preset options use the sRGB color space, and apply sharpening and tone control. To maximize image quality, I strongly recommend that you use the Custom option. As described later, no single level of sharpening or tone control is universally applicable. Furthermore, this is the only way you can select color mode II (Adobe RGB) on the D50, which is the mode you will want to use to express the widest range of colors in your pictures.

To select any of the Optimize Image controls, open the Shooting Menu and navigate to the Optimize image option and press ⊙ on the multi-selector switch to select it. This opens a page with a list of the controls. Use ⊙ to scroll to the required control then press ⊙ to select it.

If you select Custom, this action will open a further menu from which you can set each control option by pressing the ⊙ , scroll to the setting you require and select it by pressing ⊙ . Finally, navigate to Done and press ⊙ to lock your settings. If you do not carry out this last step the settings will not be saved.

*Sharpening:* This is a process applied to digital data that increases the apparent sharpness (acuity) of a picture. This is not a method for rescuing an out-of-focus picture. Remember, once out-of-focus always out-of-focus! Sharpening is used to correct certain side effects of converting light into digital data. This can cause distinct edges between colors, tones, and objects in a digital picture to look poorly defined or fuzzy. The D50 uses a technique that identifies an edge by analyzing the differences between neighboring pixel values. Then the process lightens the pixels immediately adjacent to the brighter side of the edge, and darkens the pixels adjacent to the dark side of the edge. This causes an increase of local contrast around the edge that makes it look sharper.

The D50 offers seven levels of image sharpening:

**A**  **Auto**—the D50 applies a level of sharpening that varies according to how the camera analyzes the image data.

*Note:* Nikon gives no indication as to the sharpening parameters the D50 applies at this setting.

◇ 0  **Normal**—apparently the camera applies a moderate amount of sharpening. I say, "apparently" because again Nikon does not provide specific values for the level of sharpening.

◇-2  **Low**—sharpening level is slightly less than Medium Low.

◇-1 **Medium Low**—a lesser amount of sharpening is applied than Normal.

◇+1 **Medium High**—sharpening level is slightly higher than Normal.

◇+2 **High**—the D50 applies an aggressive level of sharpening.

◈  **None**—no sharpening is applied to the image data.

**Hint:** No single level of sharpening is suitable for all picture-taking situations. Likewise, the level of sharpening should also be based on your ultimate intention for the image, (i.e.: display on a web page, publication in a book or magazine, or a print for framing).

It is often preferable to apply sharpening during post-processing on a computer, so I would make the following suggestions when shooting with the D50:

• For general photography, using JPEG format files, set sharpening to Low or Medium Low.
• If you shoot in the NEF file format, set sharpening to None.

*Note:* Although the data in a NEF file is not sharpened by the D50, the sharpening level that is set will be stored in the file's EXIF data, which means that sharpening can be applied when you convert the image in another application.

On those occasions when you need to expedite the output of pictures for publishing on a web page or in newsprint, setting the sharpening level to Normal or Medium High is probably prudent, as it will save valuable time in post processing.

*Tone Compensation:* Tone compensation (contrast control would be a better name!) allows you to adjust the contrast of an image. It works by applying a curve control similar to those used in post processing applications that alter the distribution of tones from the sensor data to fit the selected contrast range as defined by a contrast curve.

**A    Auto**—the D50 uses its Matrix metering system to assess the differences between the levels of brightness in the scene. If these are significant the camera assumes the scene has high contrast and applies a compensation to lower it. Conversely if scene contrast is assessed to be low, the D50 will increase image contrast.

◑ 0   **Normal**—the D50 applies a standard contrast curve that produces images with contrast between the extremes of Low and High contrast.

◑-2   **Low Contrast**—this setting produces images with noticeably less overall contrast, which can affect the density of very dark tones with the result that they lack depth.

◑-1   **Medium Low**—image contrast is slightly lower than Normal.

*Note:* If you expect to process your pictures in the computer, consider setting Low contrast as it is easier to increase contrast than reduce it.

80

◑+1 **Medium High** —image contrast is slightly higher than Normal.

◑+2 **High Contrast**—image contrast is boosted, producing images with deep, rich blacks and pure white, with a reduced tonal graduation between these two extremes. However, there is a risk that highlight detail will be burnt out.

◑✐ **Custom**—this option is only applicable if you have access to Nikon Capture 4.1 (or later) software, because it allows you to write your own contrast curve and upload it to the camera.

### Color Mode
The D50 offers a choice of three different color modes, or color spaces. These determine the range of colors in the image and how they will be interpreted. Select a color mode based on how you intend to use the image.

*Mode Ia (sRGB)*: This is the setting that Nikon recommends for portrait pictures.

*Mode II (Adobe RGB)*: This color mode offers a wider gamut of colors than either of the two sRGB modes (Ia and IIIa). It is the mode most often utilized by photographers because it provides the greatest number of options when it comes to the subsequent use of the image. You can always covert an Adobe RGB image to sRGB, but going from sRGB to Adobe RGB will not give you as good of a result. With this color mode there is a tendency for colors to look dull when displayed on a computer monitor, its full benefits will not be revealed until you make a print.

*Mode IIIa (sRGB)*: This setting default enhances the rendition of green and blue. Nikon recommends that it be used for nature or landscape shots.

The two sRGB color modes use a restricted gamut of colors most appropriate for display on a computer monitor. They produce rich, saturated colors but with an overall reduction in tonal range. If you are shooting pictures specifically for web-site use, or using a direct printing method with no intention of post-processing, sRGB may be a good choice. Otherwise, I recommend using the Adobe RGB color mode because it gives you more subtle control of image color.

*Note:* Although the D50 system records images in Mode II (Adobe RGB) based on EXIF and DCF, it does not strictly con-firm with these standards so it may be necessary to select the color space manually for the device or application in use.

*Note:* JPEGs taken in Mode II with the D50s are EXIF 2.21 and DCF 2.0 compliant. Applications and printers that sup-port these standards will select this color space automatically.

**Hint:** It is essential that your image-processing application be set to the same Adobe RGB color space you're shooting with, otherwise the application will more than likely assign its own default color space and you will lose control over the rendition of color.

**Saturation**

Adjusting the saturation changes the overall vividness of color (chroma) without affecting the brightness (luminance) of an image.

⊗0 **Normal**: This is the default setting and is probably the option to use for most situations, since the camera offers very limited control compared with a post-processing appli-cation.

⊗- **Moderate**: The vividness of colors is reduced but Nikon provides no information as to the level of adjustment that is applied.

⊗+ **Enhanced**: The vividness of colors is increased but Nikon provides no information as to the level of adjustment that is applied.

## Hue

The color model used by the D50 to produce images is based on combinations of red, green, and blue light. By mixing any two of these, a variety of different colors can be produced. If the third color is introduced, the hue of the color is altered. The proportions of these colors determine the warmth or coolness of the color.

The D50's Hue control allows you to manage the warmth or coolness of colors by setting an adjustment of +/- 9° in increments of 3°. For example, if the level of red and green data is increased relative to the blue data, the hue shifts (positive adjustment) to a warmer (red/yellow) rendition. If you apply a negative adjustment, the hue shifts to a cooler (blue/violet) rendition.

**Hint:** Both saturation and hue can be controlled to a far greater degree using an image processing application on a computer. I would recommend that both of these controls be left set to Normal and 0° respectively.

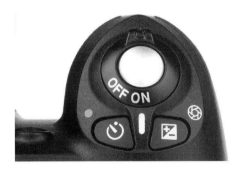

*Pressing the shutter release button half way down activates both the metering and the autofocus systems.*

## Shutter Release

The camera's shutter release is located, conventionally, on the right, top of the camera. If the D50 is switched ON light pressure on the shutter release (pressing it halfway down), will activate the metering system and initiate autofocus. Once you release the button, the camera remains active for a fixed period, the duration of which depends on the selection made within Custom Setting-18 (8-seconds at the default setting).

If you continue to press the shutter release button through its full range of travel, the shutter mechanism will operate and an exposure will be made. The short delay between the time you press the button and when the shutter opens is usually referred to as "shutter lag." The lag time of the D50, approximately 100 milliseconds. However, the release of the shutter may be delayed further if certain features and functions are in operation at the time the button is pressed. The following are some of the causes of shutter delay:

• The capacity of the D50's buffer memory is probably the most common cause of shutter delay. It does not matter whether you shoot in single frame or continuous mode (see page 90); once the buffer memory is full, the D50 must write data to the memory card before additional exposures can be made. As soon as sufficient space is available in the buffer memory for another image, the shutter can be released.

• If the camera is set to Single-servo AF mode, the shutter is disabled until the D50 has acquired focus. In low light or low contrast scenes the autofocus system can often take longer to achieve focus (see page XX), adding to the delay.

• In low-light situations, in Single-servo AF mode the D50 will activate the AF-assist lamp, provided it has been instructed to do so via Custom Setting-7.

• The red-eye reduction function, which is one of the camera's flash modes, causes a significant one-second delay between pressing the shutter release button and the exposure being made. During this time a lamp is activated—reducing the size of a subject's eye pupils—then the shutter opens and the Speedlight flash fires completing the exposure.

*Press the mode button on the upper left of the back of the camera and turn the command dial to choose your desired shooting mode.*

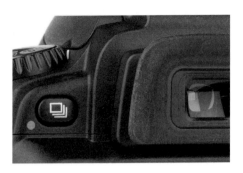

## Shooting Modes

Unlike a 35mm camera, the D50 does not have to transport film after each exposure, so in that sense it does not have a traditional motor drive. However, the shutter mechanism still has to be cycled. The camera offers two shooting modes: single-frame and continuous, plus a self-timer option, and a remote shutter release feature.

To set the shooting mode, hold down the  Mode button, located to the left of the viewfinder eyepiece and rotate the command dial until the desired icon: ⓢ Single-frame, ⌷ Continuous appears in the control panel. Release the button to select the mode.

### ⓢ Single-Frame

A single image is recorded each time the shutter release button is pressed. To make another exposure, the button must be pressed again; you can continue to do so until the buffer memory is full. At this point you must wait for data to be written to the memory card unless the memory card becomes full. You do not have to completely remove your finger from the shutter release button between frames. By raising it slightly after each exposure, while maintaining a slight downward pressure on the shutter release button, you can keep the camera active and be ready for the next shot.

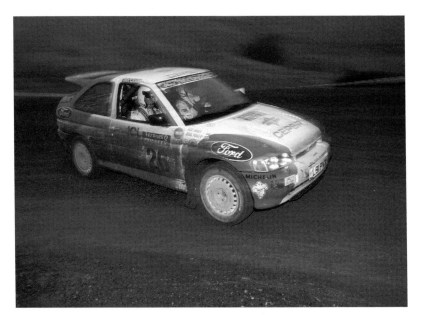

*In Single-servo AF mode the camera will activate its AF-assist lamp in low-light situations if it has been activated in Custom Setting-7. When determining whether to activate AF-assist, keep in mind that it causes a slight delay in the release of the shutter.*

**Hint:** If you want to take a rapid sequence of pictures in Single-frame mode avoid stabbing your finger down on the shutter release button. Keep a light pressure on it and roll you finger over the top of the button in a smooth action. This will reduce the risk of camera shake spoiling your pictures.

 **Continuous**

In this mode if you press and hold the shutter release button down, the D50 will continue to record images up to a maximum rate of 2.5 frames per second (fps). Nikon quotes this 2.5 fps rate based on the D50 being set to manual focus, manual exposure, and a minimum shutter speed of 1/250th second. It is important to remember that buffer capacity, auto-exposure modes, and autofocus (particularly in low-light) can, and often does, reduce the frame rate significantly.

*Note:* All pictures taken in continuous mode are recorded in the orientation of the first frame in the sequence. This applies even if you have activated the Rotate All option within the Playback menu or changed the orientation of the D50 as you shoot a series of pictures.

 **Self-Timer**

The D50 offers a self-timer function, set by pressing the ⟳ button, with variable delay. Many users automatically associate this feature with taking self-portrait pictures as the delay allows the photographer time to get in position in the composition. Personally, I find this mode more useful for releasing the shutter without having to touch the camera and thereby risk causing camera shake.

The duration of the self-timer delay is set via Custom Setting-19 (there are options for 2, 5, 10, or 20 seconds). After you press the shutter release, Self-timer Mode activates and the AF-assist Lamp, located on the front right of the camera, flashes until two seconds before the exposure is made, at which point the lamp remains on constantly as a warning that the picture is about to be taken.

Here are some tips for getting good results when using the self-timer:

• When the D50 is used remotely and not against the photographer's eye, light will enter the viewfinder and adversely influence exposure settings. Therefore, you must fit the DK-5 eyepiece cover supplied with the camera (see pages 108 for more details.)

• The D50 will attempt to acquire focus as soon as you press the shutter release, so if you (or someone else) are standing immediately in front of the camera when this operation is activated, there is a good chance that your picture will be out of focus! Furthermore, if the camera does not acquire focus in the Self-timer mode, it will not take a picture, even in Continuous-servo AF Mode. Generally, I find the most reliable method of taking pictures with the self-timer is to select Manual focus, and prefocus the lens on the subject, or the anticipated position of the subject.

- In self-timer mode the D50 makes a single exposure and then resets itself to either single-frame or continuous mode, depending on which of the two modes was last selected before the self-timer option was selected.

## Using a Remote Release

The D50 uses the Nikon ML-L3, wireless infrared (IR) remote release that is common to other Nikon cameras such as the N65/F65 and N75/F75. Pressing the transmit button on the ML-L3 sends an IR signal to the receiver, which is mounted just below the shutter release button, and above the red flash on the finger grip. The system has a maximum effective range of approximately 16 feet (5m).

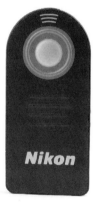

*The Nikon ML-L3 Remote Release is handy to use when a long exposure is required and you want to eliminate camera shake.*

**Hint:** Nikon claims in their instruction manual that there must be a clear, unobstructed line of sight between the ML-L3 and the D50's receiver. This is not necessarily the case, because it is quite possible to bounce the IR signal from the ML-L3 off a reflective surface such as a wall or window, which increases the usefulness of this feature.

*Note:* Nikon also supports the use of the ML-L1 wireless infrared (IR) remote release; it works in an identical manner to the ML-ML3.

The ML-L3 can be used to release the shutter in two different ways, a quick and a delayed response.

## Quick-Response Remote

The shutter is released as soon as you press the transmit button on the ML-L3 remote control. This function is set by pressing the 🕐 until 🔲 remote with immediate release appears in the control panel.

## Delayed Remote

The shutter is released with a delay of two seconds after you press the transmit button on the ML-L3 remote control. This function is set by pressing the 🕐 until 🔲 remote with delayed release appears in the control panel.

Regardless of which remote mode you choose, the D50 will automatically cancel it after a fixed period of camera inactivity. At the default setting this period is one minute, but you can also set it to 5, 10, or 15 minutes, via Custom Setting-20.

**Hint:** If you want to make extremely long exposures with the D50 you can use the **buLb** setting (Manual Exposure Mode only) in conjunction with the ML-L3. This works in both remote release modes. Used this way, **buLb** is replaced by  **- -**  and the exposure is started by the first press of the transmit button on the ML-L3, and finished with a second press of the button. A single flash of the AF-assist Lamp confirms completion of the exposure.

*Note:* The D50 will end the exposure automatically after 30 minutes.

## The Memory Buffer

The D50 has a memory buffer that provides temporary storage of image files. This allows the camera to continue recording pictures while data is written to the memory card. As soon as the memory buffer is full, the shutter release is disabled, and no further pictures can be taken until sufficient data has been moved to the memory card to make room for another image. The number of pictures that can be stored in the memory buffer depends on the settings selected for image quality and size (see following table).

## D50 Memory Buffer Capacity

| Image Quality | Image Size | Buffer Capcity[1] Long Exp. Nr - Off | Buffer Capcity[1] Long Exp. Nr - On |
|---|---|---|---|
| NEF (RAW) | - | 4 | 3 |
| JPEG Large | L | 9 | 7 |
| JPEG Large | M | 10 | 8 |
| JPEG Large | S | 19 | 17 |
| JPEG Normal | L | 12 | 10 |
| JPEG Normal | M | 16 | 14 |
| JPEG Normal | S | 27 | 25 |
| JPEG Basic | L | 19 | 17 |
| JPEG Basic | M | 27 | 25 |
| JPEG Basic | S | 49 | 47 |
| NEF + JPEG Basic | L | 4 | 3 |

[1] – *These figures represent the maximum number of pictures that can be stored in the buffer memory. The actual number of pictures that can be taken may be lower depending on the status, of the buffer memory, and the make and model of the memory card.*

If the Long Exposure Noise Reduction feature, set from the Shooting Menu, is active (see table), the number of pictures that can be stored in the memory buffer is reduced, slightly.

The number of images that can be stored in the memory buffer, at the set quality and size, is shown in the exposure counter brackets in both the Control Panel and viewfinder while the shutter release is depressed. For example, [r04] indicates that four images can be stored in the memory buffer.

## The Autofocus System

The D50's autofocus (AF) system is derived from the systems in the N80/F80 film camera and D70/70s digital SLR. It uses five sensors, arranged in a cross formation. Their approximate position is indicated by the five pairs of brackets marked on the viewfinder screen. The actual area covered by each sensor is more linear than the area delineated by the brackets (see illustration of viewfinder below). These sensors measure contrast in the subject, and signals are sent to the focusing motor in the camera, or the motor built-in to AF-S and AF-I type lenses. These motors cause the point of focus to be shifted until the maximum level of contrast is attained, at which point the subject should be in sharp focus.

*The center cross-type sensor is surrounded by the four single direction sensors.*

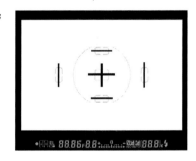

It is very important to understand that of the five autofocus sensors, the central one differs significantly from the other four. The center sensor is a cross-type that is equally sensitive to vertical and horizontal patterns or detail. Generally, the other four sensors are only sensitive to detail or patterns in a single direction. Consequently, these sensors are not as effective at acquiring focus in subjects with detail or patterns in the same orientation as the sensor.

Furthermore, the center sensor area (cross-type) has two sets of sensors, which increase its ability to work in a wider range of light levels. This sensor area is far more sensitive in low light than the single line-type sensors in the other four sensor areas. Once focus is achieved the confirmation signal (●) appears in the viewfinder display.

## Focusing Options

The D50 has two focusing options: Autofocus (AF) and Manual Focus (M). The AF mode switch, located on the side of the lens mount below the lens release button, is used to select these:

***Autofocus (AF):*** If you select autofocus (AF), the lens is focused automatically when the shutter release button is partially or completely depressed. Depending on which focus mode is selected, the shutter will either not fire until focus is acquired, or it will fire even if the camera has not found focus. As soon as focus has been achieved, and provided the shutter release remains half way down, the D50 will either lock focus at that distance, or begin to track a moving subject until the shutter release is pressed fully.

***Manual Focus (M):*** The manual focus (M) option requires the user to physically turn the focusing ring of the lens to achieve focus. There is no restriction on when the shutter can be fired, and the focus confirmation signal still functions, which is particularly useful in low light or low contrast. The focus mode selector switch must be set to M with most AF-Nikkor lenses. However, if the lens you are using has a switch that allows you to set an M/A (manual/autofocus) mode, you can leave the lens set to M/A and you need only touch the focusing ring and the lens can be focused manually. As soon as you release the focusing ring it will revert to autofocus operation. The focus mode selector switch on the D50 can be left set to AF. Despite the autofocusing capabilities for the D50, there are occasions when focusing manually is preferable:

- In close-up photography, controlling the depth-of-field is often critical, so accurate focusing is essential. Since many subjects are relatively static, by focusing manually you can place the plane of focus with precision.
- In numerous sports, competitors pass through a fixed point such as a section of track, a jump, or the finish line. By manually pre-focusing on these positions and releasing the shutter just a fraction of a second before the sub-

ject reaches them, you can capture the peak moment in action shots.

- You may have some earlier manual focus Nikkor lenses that you want to use with the D50.

*Note:* If you attach a non-CPU lens to the camera, the TTL metering system will not function.

- There are circumstances in which the AF system may become unreliable (see page 99 "Limitations of the AF System"); in these cases switch to Manual focus and use the electronic rangefinder as a focusing aid. When focus has been achieved, the focus confirmation signal (●) will light up in the viewfinder.

## Autofocus Modes

The camera has three distinct focus modes, which are selected via Custom Setting-2. They are: Automatic Autofocus (AF-A), Single-servo Autofocus (AF-S), and Continuous-servo Autofocus (AF-C).

*AF-A—Automatic Autofocus:* This is an entirely new feature used in the D50 for the first time. The camera selects either AF-S or AF-C mode automatically depending on the shooting conditions, and whether it detects that the subject is moving or stationary.

*AF-S—Single-Servo Autofocus:* While the shutter release is pressed halfway down, the D50 focuses and then locks at the focus distance. The shutter can only be released once focus has been acquired (check the in-focus signal is displayed in the viewfinder). If the subject was moving when the shutter release was first pressed half way, the camera will track the subject until focus is achieved, and then the shutter can be released (see page 94 "Predictive Focus Tracking"). If the subject stops moving before the shutter is released, the D50 focuses, and then locks at the focus distance.

*AF-C—Continuous-Servo Autofocus:* While the shutter release is pressed halfway down, the D50 focuses continuously. In addition to tracking a subject that was originally moving when the shutter release was first pressed half way, AF-C mode will also initiate tracking if the camera detects that the subject has begun to move after the shutter release was first pressed.

There is a fundamental difference between the latter two modes. In AF-S, referred to by Nikon as "focus priority," the shutter cannot be released until focus has been acquired. Conversely, in AF-C, which Nikon calls "release priority," the shutter will operate immediately upon pressing the shutter release all the way down, regardless of whether focus has been achieved. Some photographers mistakenly believe that if you release the shutter before the camera has apparently focused, the picture will be out of focus. In fact the camera is often capable of predicting where the subject will be within the frame and shifting the focus point accordingly, all within the split second between the mirror lifting and the shutter opening. Even if the camera's calculations are still slightly out, the depth of field can often make up for minor focusing errors. In AF-C, it is imperative that you allow the camera time to establish a starting point for the focusing action by pressing the shutter release half way and holding long enough for it to do so, otherwise it is likely the picture will be out of focus.

*Note:* AF-S and AF-C can only be selected by the user in P, S, A, and M exposure modes. The selected AF mode icon is shown in the control panel (if AF-A is selected no icon is displayed).

*Predictive Focus Tracking:* It is important to understand the distinction between how the autofocus tracking system works in AF-S and AF-C modes. In AF-S mode, Predictive Focus Tracking is initiated if the camera detects the subject is moving at the time the shutter release is first pressed half way. If the subject stops, focus will be acquired and the lens locked at that focus distance. Any subsequent movement by the subject will have no effect of the AF system. In AF-C mode, predictive focus tracking is initiated regardless of whether the subject was moving at the time the shutter release was first pressed half way. If the subject was static, or moving at this point in time, and it subsequently stops, the D50 will acquire but continue to monitor focus. If the subject begins to move again, the camera will commence focus tracking once more to follow the subject

## Focus Area Modes

The D50 has three modes that define how the five autofocus sensors are used by the camera. These are known as the AF area modes, and are set via Custom Setting-3 (see page 147 for more details).

[ ɪ ]  *Single Area AF:* The D50 uses the autofocus area you select for focusing. In this mode the camera takes no part in choosing which sensor to use. The selected area is highlighted in the viewfinder.

[·ᵤ·]  *Dynamic Area AF:* To start, the D50 uses the autofocus area you select for focusing, but if it detects that the subject is moving, the camera evaluates information from the other AF areas and shifts to another sensor if necessary. The selected area is highlighted in the viewfinder and remains highlighted even if the subject leaves it.

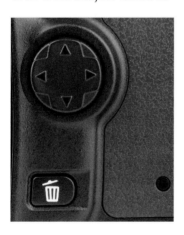

*In order to change Focus Area modes, you must release the focus selector lock by shifting it upward. Use the multi-selector switch to select a new AF area mode.*

To select the AF area that the D50 will use as the initial focus point:

1. If the camera is not already active press the shutter release half way and let go of it.
2. Press the multi-selector switch up, down, left, or right to change between the five sensors.

**◼** *Closest-subject priority AF:* The camera always focuses with the sensor area that detects the object closest to the camera. I say "object" rather than "subject" because this is frequently not the subject! The user has no control over which sensor area is used for focusing.

## AF System Overview

If you are new to Nikon's AF system it will take a while to get used to the functionality of Focus Mode and Focus Area Mode. Therefore, you may wish to re-read the sections above and refer to the following table that sets out, in summary, the various autofocus operations.

## AF System Operation

| Custom Setting-2 (Autofocus) | Custom Setting-3 (AF-area Mode) | Control panel | View-finder | Active focus area | Focus-Area selection |
|---|---|---|---|---|---|
| AF-A AF-S AF-C | Single area | [ ⚬ ] | [ ⚬ ] | Shown in viewfinder and control panel | Manual |
| | Dynamic area | [ +⚬+ ] | [ ·⚬· ] | Shown in viewfinder and control panel | Manual |
| | Closest subject | [ +++ ] | [ ··· ] | Not shown | Automatic |

## AF-Assist Lamp

The D50 has a small, built-in white light known as the AF-assist Lamp, which is designed to facilitate autofocusing in low light conditions. Whatever the intentions were of the D50's design team, this feature is largely superfluous!

*The built-in AF-assist lamp is located on the front of the camera.*

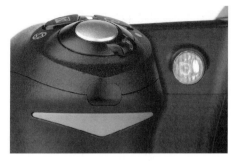

Here are a few reasons why you may as well go to Custom Setting-7 and select the option that cancels the lamp's operation.

- The lamp only works if you have an autofocus lens attached to the camera, the focus option set to AF-S (Single-servo) with either the center focus area, or closest-subject priority active.

- It is only usable with focal lengths between 24mm–200mm

- The operating range is restricted to between 1 feet 8 inches to 9 feet 10 inches (0.5–3.0m)

- Due to the lamp's location, many lenses obstruct its output, particularly if they have a lens hood attached.

- It is disabled with all VR-type telephoto zoom lenses, and the AF-S and AF-D versions of the 80-200mm f/2.8 Nikkor lenses.

- The lamp overheats quite quickly (6 to 8 exposures in rapid succession is usually sufficient) and will automatically shut down to allow it to cool. Plus, at this level of use it also drains battery power.

## Focus Lock

Once the D50 has achieved focus it is possible to lock the autofocus system as follows:

*AF-S—Single-Servo Autofocus:* Pressing the shutter release halfway will activate autofocus, which will lock automatically as soon as focus is acquired, and remain locked at the same focus distance until you let go of the shutter release button. Alternatively, you can lock focus if you press and hold the button. You no longer have to press the shutter release button.

*AF-C—Continuous-Servo Autofocus:* The autofocus system remains active, constantly adjusting the focus point, while you press and hold the shutter release button halfway down. Press and hold the button to retain focus lock. You no longer have to press the shutter release.

*Custom Setting-14 can be used to designate the operation of the ever-important AE/AF Lock Button.*

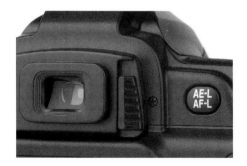

## Limitations of the AF System

Although the autofocus system of the D50 is very effective, there are some circumstances or conditions that limit its performance. These are: low light, low contrast, highly reflective surfaces, very small subjects, focusing on very fine detail, geometric patterns, and very high-contrast subjects.

If the autofocus system continuously hunts (i.e. the focus shifts back and forth without locking on to a subject), switch to M, manual focus, and use the electronic rangefinder as a focusing aid.

# Exposure

Regardless of whether you are content to let the D50 make decisions about exposure or you prefer to take control of your camera and make them for yourself, it is essential to understand how the camera sees, evaluates, and processes light.

### Sensitivity

When you bought a roll of film you had to make a decision about which ISO (sensitivity) rating to use for the expected lighting conditions. Once, once loaded in the camera, the entire roll of film had to be exposed at the same sensitivity value. One of the great advantages of digital photography is that digital cameras generally allow you to adjust the sensitivity from picture to picture. The D50 is no exception, offering sensitivity settings (in ISO equivalent values) from 200 to 1600 in increments of one EV (exposure value). In addition to this, the camera has two features that attempt to adjust this sensitivity value according to the light conditions.

### D50 Sensitivity Options: ISO Control / ISO Auto

| Operation / Exposure Mode | All DVP Modes | P, S, A, and M |
|---|---|---|
| Camera selects sensitivity | ISO Control: ON (CS-9) | Not Available |
| User selects sensitivity | ISO Control: OFF (CS-9) ISO Auto: OFF (CS-10) | ISO Auto: OFF (CS-10) |
| User selects sensitivity but camera may adjust it | ISO Control: OFF (CS-9) ISO Auto: ON (CS-10) | ISO Auto: ON (CS-10) |

I use the word sensitivity advisedly since the CCD in the D50 actually has a fixed sensitivity, equivalent to ISO 200. The higher ISO values are achieved by amplifying the data from the sensor within the camera's analog-to-digital converter (ADC).

*Setting the ISO Value:* To set the sensitivity value on the D50 you can take two different routes:

- Open the Shooting menu and scroll to ISO, press the ⊙ to open the sub-menu of values, then scroll down using the Multi Selector Switch, highlight the required value and press the ⊙ again to set it.
- As an alternative you can adjust the sensitivity (ISO) by pressing and holding the ISO button on the rear of the camera, and then turning the main command dial. The selected value is displayed in the control panel.

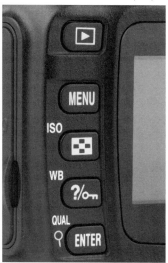

*There are often multiple ways to select a function or setting by using the various buttons and dials. One way to choose your ISO is to hold the ISO Button while turning the command dial.*

There is a further analogy with film in that the images show an increasing amount of digital noise at higher sensitivity settings. However, this noise is not random like the distribution of grain in film, and reduces the tonality of pictures. As the sensitivity value is hiked higher and higher, so the saturation of color and level of image contrast are reduced.

For the optimum image quality use ISO 200 on the D50. At the ISO 400 setting image quality is virtually indistinguishable from ISO 200 with a hint of higher noise levels. Quality at the ISO 800 setting is still extremely good, although there is a perceptible increase in noise (graininess) and a reduction in both saturation and contrast, with the possibility that colors may shift slightly. The highest setting of ISO 1600 is more than usable with image quality affected in the same way as it is at ISO 800 but to a greater degree.

**Hint:** If the light level begins to drop as you shoot, you can either raise the ISO setting or use a longer shutter speed. Confronted with this situation, I recommend putting the camera on a tripod and selecting a longer shutter speed in combination with the long exposure Noise Reduction feature available in the Shooting menu.

*ISO Control:* This feature supplements the highly automated functionality of the DVP exposure modes; if you are content using these I expect that you will not be concerned at leaving CS-9 ISO Control at its default setting of ON.

*ISO Auto:* I dislike this option so much that I will begin this section by suggesting you ignore it, completely! Why? Well, it is important to understand that it does not work in quite the way I think most users expect.

In Auto Multi Program (P), Aperture-Priority (A), and the seven Digital Vari-Program modes, the sensitivity will not change until the exposure reaches the limits of the shutter speed range. The upper limit is always 1/8000 second but the lower limit can be adjusted within Custom Setting-5, in increments of one-stop, between 1/4000 and 1/125 second.

In Shutter-Priority auto exposure mode (S), the sensitivity is shifted when the exposure reaches the limit of the available aperture range. Indeed, this is the only exposure mode with which ISO Auto might be useful, because it will raise the sensitivity setting and thus maintain the pre-selected shutter speed, which in this mode is probably critical to the success of the picture.

In Manual exposure mode (M), the sensitivity is shifted if the selected shutter speed and aperture cannot attain a correct exposure as indicated by central "0" in the analog display of the viewfinder.

The biggest problem with the ISO Auto Mode is that you can never be sure of exactly what sensitivity value the D50 has set. Although a warning appears in the Control Panel to indicate this function is active, there is no indication of what value (ISO) has been set.

**TTL Metering**
The D50 has three metering options that will be familiar if you have used a Nikon AF camera before. To select a metering mode, open Custom Setting-13, highlight one of the three metering options, and press (insert multi selector switch right arrow icon) to select it. The appropriate icon will be displayed in the control panel.

 *Matrix Metering:* The metering pattern for this mode divides most of the image area into a matrix, or series of segments, and assesses the difference in brightness between them. (The extreme edges of the frame area are not included in this metering pattern.) These values are compared against a database of brightness reference patterns so that the camera can compute an exposure setting. The meter in the D50 is a very sophisticated tool that uses a 420-pixel CCD located in the viewfinder to measure light values. In fact it is a modified version of the same system used in Nikon's flagship D2-series digital SLR cameras.

**Hint:** It is essential to remember that every TTL metering system measures reflected light, and is calibrated to give a correct exposure for a mid-tone gray. You must make sure that the part of the scene you meter represents a mid-tone, otherwise you will need to adjust the recommended exposure value.

When using a D-type or G-type Nikkor lens, you will gain the most from the D50's metering capabilities. These lenses provide additional information about the focus dis-

102

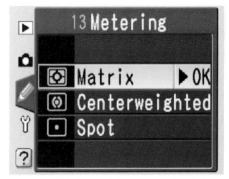

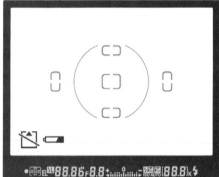

*Matrix metering gives extra consideration to the area surrounding the active AF sensor because it is logical to assume that the subject is located in this part of the frame.*

tance, which assists the D50 in estimating the sort of picture you are taking by providing information on where in the frame the subject is likely to be (the camera assumes the subject is in the plane of sharp focus).

Matrix metering uses four principle factors when calculating an exposure value:

* The overall brightness level of the scene
* The ratio of brightness between the matrix pattern segments
* The active focus area, which suggests the position of the subject in the frame
* The focused distance, provided by the lens (D- or G-type only)

**Hint:** The camera is biased to preserve highlight values over shadow values, because, like transparency film, once a highlight detail is overexposed it is lost and no amount of subsequent image manipulation will recover it. However, it is possible to recover shadow detail from underexposed areas. Therefore, if the scene you photograph has a wide contrast range (large variation in brightness) do not be surprised if it looks as though it has been underexposed. Fortunately, the D50 has a couple of features that help you to evaluate an exposure: the histogram and highlight warning. For more information see pages 119-122.

*Center-Weighted Metering:* The center-weighted metering pattern harkens back to the very first TTL metering systems used in Nikon SLR film cameras. In these cameras the frame area was usually divided in a 60:40 ratio with the exposure measurement bias placed on the central portion of the frame. While this is similar in theory, the D50 actually uses a stronger ratio of 75:25, with 75% of the exposure reading based on the central area of the frame and the remaining 25% based on the outer area. The principal metering area corresponds to the 8mm-diameter circle marked in the center of the D50's focusing screen.

*The area designated by the circle is given 75% emphasis in calculating the exposure in Center-Weighted Metering.*

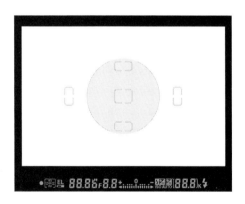

**Hint:** Center-weighted metering is the least accurate of the three metering patterns available on the D50. Matrix will do an excellent job in most situations and for particularly tricky lighting, the spot meter is more useful than the center-weighted pattern.

*Spot Metering:* spot metering is extremely useful for measuring a highly specific area of a scene. For example, with a subject against a virtually black background (which would more than likely cause the Matrix metering system to overexpose), the Spot meter allows you to take a reading from the subject without it being influenced by the background. The Spot metering function of the D50 centers a circle, approximately 2.5 mm in diameter, on one of the five AF-sensor area brackets, so the metering area is actually larger than the AF-sensor bracket. The metering area corresponds to the active AF-sensor area, unless closest subject priority is selected, in which case only the center AF-sensor area is used.

**Hint:** In Dynamic Area AF, the D50 will attempt to follow a moving subject and may shift focus control between any of the five AF-sensor areas. If this occurs, the spot metering also shifts, following the active AF-sensor area. If in doubt, switch to Manual focus as the D50 will always use the user selected active AF-sensor area for spot metering.

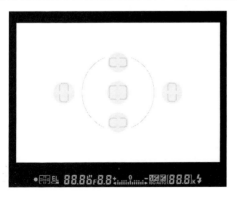

*The spot meter uses the small 2.5 mm circular area surrounding the active AF sensor to measure light for exposure calculation.*

*The Mode Dial*

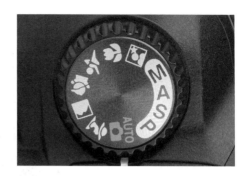

## Exposure Modes

The D50 has four, principal exposure modes in addition to the Digital Vari-Programs offered by the camera (see page 49 for more information).

To select an exposure mode, turn the Mode Dial on the left top of the camera to the required position (P, A, S, or M).

*Note:* For P, A, or S modes to operate, you must have a CPU lens attached to the camera. Attaching a non-CPU lens will cause **F- -** to appear in the viewfinder display and control panel. The shutter release is also disabled. You can use manual exposure mode with non-CPU lenses and set the aperture value via the aperture ring on the lens. However, the TTL metering system of the D50 will not work.

*P—Auto Multi-Program:* Program mode (P), as it is often referred to, automatically adjusts both the shutter speed and lens aperture to produce a correctly exposed image. The camera's response is based upon the meter reading and the analysis of predetermined values stored in the camera. The D50 also takes into consideration the focal length of the lens, which it divides into three broad groups, wide-angle/standard (<70mm), short/medium telephoto (70-200mm), and telephoto (>200mm). Using this information the D50 will keep the lens open at its maximum aperture until a threshold shutter speed can be attained; thereafter the aperture and shutter speed values are increased together. For wide-angle/standard focal lengths, the threshold speed is 1/8 second, for short/medium telephoto it is 1/125 second, and for telephoto it is 1/1000 second.

106

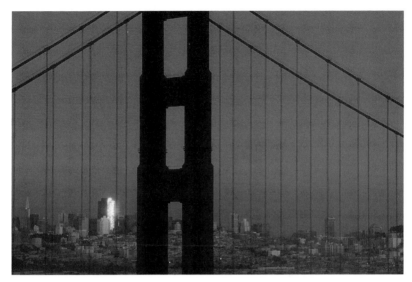

*You may find Manual exposure mode the best choice for scenes with unusual reflectance such as this.*

If you decide that a particular combination chosen by the camera is not preferable, you can take advantage of the camera's flexible program feature and override the Program mode settings by turning the command dial when the camera meter is activated. 🅿 appears in the control panel, but there is no indication in the viewfinder that you have overridden the mode, other than the altered shutter speed and aperture values. The two values change in tandem, so the overall exposure remains the same (increasing the shutter speed decreases the aperture).

**Hint:** If you use the flexible program feature the camera will remain locked to its new settings for shutter speed and aperture, even if the meter auto-powers off, and you switch it on again by pressing the shutter release halfway. To cancel the override, you must turn the command dial until (insert flexible Program icon) is no longer displayed in the control panel. Alternatively, change the exposure mode, turn the power switch to OFF, or perform a camera reset.

**Hint:** Program mode can be handy for other family members or quick snapshot photography. However, in my opinion, Program mode is little better than the Digital Vari-Program modes because you relinquish control of exposure to the camera. If you want to make informed decisions about shutter speed and aperture for creative photography, it is not the best choice.

*A—Aperture-Priority Auto Exposure:* In this mode the photographer selects an aperture value and the D50 chooses a shutter speed to produce an appropriate exposure. The aperture is controlled by the command dial (default) and is changed in increments of 1/3-stop (default). The shutter speed the D50 selects will also change in increments of 1/3-stop (default).

*S—Shutter-Priority Auto Exposure:* In this mode the photographer sets the shutter speed and the D50 automatically chooses the aperture to produce an appropriate exposure. The shutter speed is controlled by the command dial and is changed in increments of 1/3-stop (default). The aperture value the D50 selects will also change in increments of 1/3-stop (default).

*Note:* Use Custom Setting-11 if you want changes in A, and S modes to be done in an increment of 1/2-stop.

**Hint:** If you use the D50 remotely, without having your eye to the viewfinder when you make an exposure, as you would when taking a self-portrait or using the ML-L3 Remote Control to release the shutter, you must cover over the viewfinder eyepiece. The metering sensor of the D50 is located within the viewfinder-head; therefore, light entering the viewfinder eyepiece will affect exposures made in DVP P, A, and S, modes. Nikon supplies the D50 with the DK-5 eyepiece cover for this purpose, but to use it the rubber eyecup fitted on the camera must be removed first. Personally, I find attaching the DK-5 a fuss, so I keep a small square of thick, black felt fabric in my camera bag, and drape this over the camera to block light from the viewfinder eyepiece.

***M—Manual Exposure:*** This mode offers the photographer total control over exposure, and is probably the most useful if you want to learn more about the effect of shutter speed and aperture on the final appearance of your pictures. You choose and control both the shutter speed and lens aperture, while an analog display shown in the viewfinder indicates the level of exposure your settings would produce. Turn the command dial to adjust the shutter speed. To adjust the aperture value press and hold the 🄯 button and turning the command dial.

## Auto-Exposure Lock

If you take a meter reading in any of the three auto-exposure modes, P, A, or S, and recompose the picture after taking this reading, the metering area will fall on an another part of the scene and may produce a different exposure value.

The D50 allows you to lock the initial exposure reading while you reframe and take the picture. Start by positioning the part of the scene you want to meter within the appropriate metering area (one the five AF-sensor area brackets for spot metering, and the center AF-sensor bracket for center-weighted metering), press the shutter release half way to acquire a reading, and then press and hold the 🔒 Button. You can now recompose and take the picture at metered value.

***Note:*** You must ensure an appropriate selection has been made at Custom Setting-14. EL will appear in the viewfinder display while this function is active.

**Hint:** While this function works with all three metering modes, it is generally most effective with center-weighted and spot metering. These two modes are most useful in difficult lighting conditions, when a more accurate exposure reading can be to taken from a specific area of the scene, which may otherwise "fool" Matrix metering.

## Exposure Compensation

As with all TTL metering systems, the D50 works on the assumption that it is pointed at a scene with a reflectivity equivalent to mid-gray. But what does mid-gray equate to? I have it on good authority from senior engineers at Nikon that contemporary Nikon camera meters are calibrated to their own in-house standard, and not the American National Standards Institute (ANSI) as suggest by some. As a consequence, if you take a picture of a Kodak 18% gray card and look at the histogram produced by the D50, you will see the tonal peak is left-of-center (i.e. underexposed). Although subjective, my tests would indicate that the Nikon calibration target has an equivalent reflectivity of about 14% to 15%, in other words approximately 1/3-stop less than 18% gray. So bear in mind that if you use a gray card to check your exposure readings you need to adjust the exposure by about + 1/3-stop.

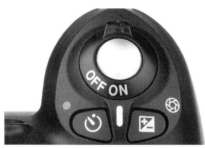

*The exposure compensation button is to the right and rear of the shutter release button.*

Many scenes will not reflect 14% to 15% of the light falling on them. For example a landscape under a blanket of fresh snowfall is going to reflect far more light than a mountain covered with black volcanic rock. Unless you compensate your exposure, both the snow and rock will be reproduced as mid-gray in your pictures.

To set a compensation factor hold down the ⊞ exposure compensation button, located to the rear and right of the shutter release button. Turn the command dial until the required value is shown in the control panel. The value is also displayed in the viewfinder while the button is held down.

*Note:* The value will change +/- by increments of 1/3 or 1/2-stop depending on which increment you have selected in CS-11.)

*Note:* The Exposure Compensation function does not operate in Manual exposure mode.

Once you have set a compensation factor it will remain locked until you hold down the 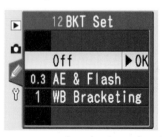 exposure compensation button and reset the value to 0.0.

**Automatic Exposure Bracketing**
It is important when shooting digital pictures to expose as accurately as you can. Overexposure causes the loss of highlight detail and underexposure degrades image quality due to electronic noise and lack of detail in dark areas.

The TTL meter of the D0 is very effective but not infallible. To increase the chances of getting the most ideal exposure in difficult lighting conditions, it is often wise to bracket exposures (take a series of pictures at slightly different settings).

The automatic exposure bracketing system in the D50 allows you to take a sequence of three exposures varied by increments of 1/3-stop or 1/2-stop. It also has a feature to bracket white balance for images shot in the JPEG standard. However, exposure and white balance values cannot be bracketed simultaneously.

In automatic exposure bracketing the D50 varies the exposure (and the flash exposure if either the built-in flash, or an external Speedlight is functioning) simultaneously over a series of three shots. The maximum range of the bracketed sequence is +/- 2EV, and this can be done by increments in multiples of either a 1/3EV, or 1/2EV subject to the selected value at Custom Setting-11.

To select automatic exposure bracketing open the Custom menu and navigate to CS-12. Highlight AE & Flash and press ☉ , a list of the available increments will then be displayed. Highlight the required value and press ☉ to select it.

The 🅑🅣🅚 🅕 icons will be displayed in the control panel, and 🅑🅣🅚 (insert exposure compensation icon) will appear in the viewfinder display.

*Note:* Bracketing will remain set even if you exchange the memory card, or switch the camera off, so be sure to cancel it once you have finished shooting by selecting OFF in CS-12.

*Note:* Bracketing is only available in P, S, A, and M exposure modes. In continuous shooting mode picture taking will stop after each sequence of three exposures.

### *Exposure Bracketing Considerations:*
- Using 🅢 single-frame mode, you have to press the Shutter Release Button to make each exposure in the bracketing sequence. At the start of a three-shot sequence the bracketing icon in the control panel will be displayed as ＋◀▥►－ . If the icon has any other configuration it indicates you are part way through a sequence.

- If you set the D50 to continuous mode, then press and hold the Shutter Release Button down, the camera will only take the three frames specified in the bracket sequence. The camera stops regardless of whether the shutter release continues to be depressed.

- If you turn the D50 OFF, or have to change the memory card during a bracketing sequence, the camera remembers which exposure values are outstanding, so when you turn the camera ON, or insert a new memory card, the sequence will resume from where it stopped.

- You can combine a bracketing sequence with a fixed exposure compensation factor. For example, if you apply an exposure compensation of +1.0EV to deal with a

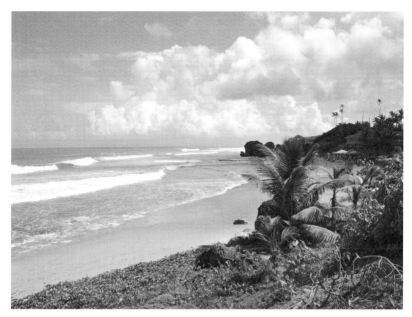

*If you are not sure which exposure will render the various elements of a scene most to your liking, try using the camera's automatic exposure bracketing feature.* ©Mimi Netzel

scene such as a snow covered landscape that comprises predominantly of light tones, and then set a bracket sequence of three-frames at an increment of 1-stop, the actual exposures you make will be at, 0, +1EV, and +2EV.

- In P, A, and M exposure modes the D50 alters the shutter speed to achieve the variation in exposure. In S exposure mode it varies the lens aperture. No alternative is availalble.

**Aperture and Depth of Field**

When a lens brings light to focus on a camera's sensor there is only ever one plane-of-focus that is critically sharp. However, in the two dimensional picture produced by the camera, there is a zone in front of and behind the plane-of-focus that is perceived to be sharp. This area of apparent sharpness is often referred to as the depth of field, and its extent is influenced by the camera-to-subject distance together with the focal length and aperture of the lens in use.

If the focal length and camera-to-subject distance are constant, depth of field will be shallower with large apertures (low f/ numbers) and deeper with small apertures (high f/ numbers). If the aperture and camera-to-subject distance are constant, depth of field will be shallower with a long focal length (telephoto range) and deeper with shorter focal length (wide-angle range). If the focal length and aperture are constant, depth of field will be greater at longer camera-to-subject distances and shallower with closer camera-to-subject distances.

Depth-of-field is an important consideration when deciding on a particular composition as it has a direct and fundamental effect on the final appearance of the picture.

***Depth-of-Field Considerations:*** Probably the most important consideration concerning depth of field is that it is less for images shot on a D50 than those shot on a film camera. This is due to the smaller size of the sensor in the D50 (23.7 x 15.6mm) compared with a 35mm film frame (24 x 36mm); the digital picture must be magnified by a greater amount compared with 35mm film to achieve any given print size. Therefore, at normal viewing distances, detail that appears to be sharp in a print (i.e. within the depth of field) made from a film-based image may no longer look sharp in a print of the same dimensions made from a digital file. If you use the depth-of-field values given in tables for lenses used with 35mm film, you will find they do not correspond to images shot on the D50, assuming the same camera-to-subject distance and focal length apply. To guarantee that the depth of field in pictures taken on

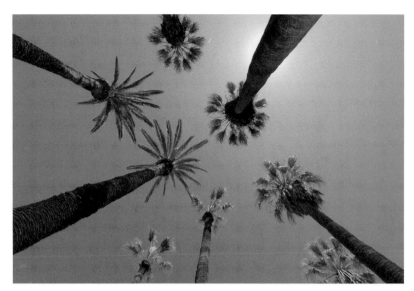

*If you want to get a deep zone of acceptable sharpness in a photo—in this case everything from the tree trunks to the leaves—use a small aperture (large f/number).*

the D50 is sufficiently deep, use the values for the next larger lens aperture. For example, if set your lens to f/16, use the depth-of-field values for f/11 with the D50.

Apart from setting a small aperture (large f/number) to maximize depth of field in a landscape picture, it is worth remembering that at mid to long focus distances the zone of apparent sharpness will extend about 1/3 in front of the point of focus and 2/3 behind it. Therefore, by placing the point of focus about a third of the way into your scene you will maximize the coverage of the depth of field of the shooting aperture.

In portrait photography, is often preferable to render the background out-of-focus so it does not distract from the subject(s). The simplest way to achieve this effect is to use a longer focal length lens (a short telephoto of 70 to 105mm is ideal) in combination with a large aperture (low f/ number).

In close-up photography, depth of field is limited, so convention suggests you set the lens to its minimum aperture (largest f/ number) value. However, I strongly recommend that you avoid doing this, because the effects of diffraction at, or near the minimum aperture of a lens cause a significant loss of image sharpness. Generally, you will achieve superior results at an aperture one-stop wider than the minimum value.

*Note:* It is likely that, even in good light, the shutter speed will be rather slow when shooting with a small lens aperture, so consider using a tripod or other camera support whenever possible.

Unlike the distribution of the depth-of-field zone for mid to long focused distances, at very short distances the depth of field extends by an equal amount in front of and behind the plane of focus. By placing the plane of focus with care you can use this fact to further maximize depth of field. Once again the ability to playback images in the LCD will allow you to review the depth of field in your composition.

## Shutter Speed Considerations

If you handhold your camera, it is worth remembering a rule of thumb concerning the minimum shutter speed that is, generally, sufficient to prevent a loss of sharpness due to camera shake. Take the reciprocal value of the lens focal length (mm), and use this as the slowest shutter speed with that lens. For example, with a focal length of 200mm, set a minimum shutter speed of 1/200th second.

*Portraits usually are most successful when the background is soft and out-of-focus. To achieve this, choose a wide aperture (small f/number), which will minimize depth of field. Then, if you focus on your subject's eyes, the portrait will be a winner!*

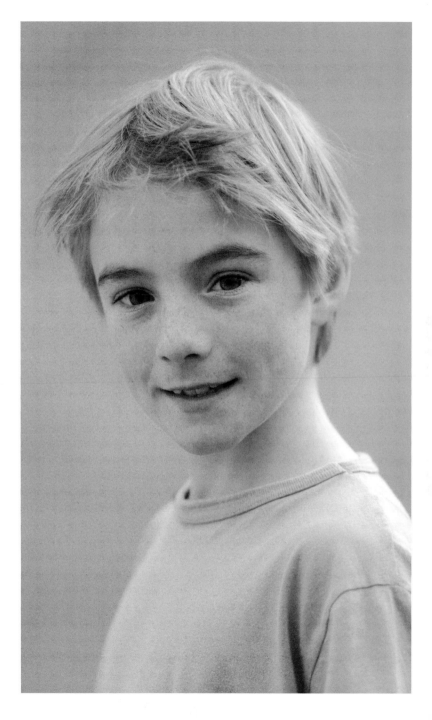

*Note:* Longer focal length lenses, and higher subject magnification in close-up photography, amplify the effects of camera shake.

The choice of shutter speed can be used for creative effect because it controls the way that motion is depicted in a photograph. Generally, fast shutter speeds are used if you wish to freeze motion in sports or action photography. Slower shutter speeds (1/30th second or longer) can be used to introduce a degree of blur that will often evoke a greater sense of movement than a subject that is rendered pin-sharp. Alternatively, you can pan the camera with the subject so that it appears relatively sharp against an increased level of blur in the background.

If you want a moving element to "disappear" in a picture of a static subject, a very long shutter speed of several seconds or more can often be very effective. While the subject is rendered properly, the moving element does not record sufficient information in any part of the frame to be visible. So next time you want to take a picture of a famous building and exclude the visitors from cluttering up your composition you know how!

## Metering

If the D50 is your first digital SLR camera, and your previous photography has been done with a 35mm camera and color negative film, you may find controlling exposure with the D50 rather more demanding. Color negative (print) film is very tolerant to exposure errors, particularly overexposure. The automated processing machines used to produce your prints are capable of correcting exposure errors over a range of -2 to +3 stops while adjusting color balance at the same time. The chances are that you never saw your exposure errors when looking at finished prints!

Controlling exposure with a digital SLR is analogous to shooting transparency (slide) film—there is virtually no margin for error. Even moderate overexposure will blow out highlight detail, leaving no usable image data in these areas. The Matrix Metering system of the D50 will attempt to hold highlight detail, but images can appear to lack contrast (look flat) and be underexposed. The easiest way of rectifying this issue is to make adjustments to the image data using the levels or a curve control curve control in an image processing program such as Adobe Photoshop.

## The Histogram and Highlights
The D50 has two very useful features that allow you to evaluate exposure after a picture has been taken.

***What is a Histogram?*** The histogram is a graphical display of the tonal values recorded by the camera. The horizontal axis represents brightness, with dark tones shown to the left and bright to the right. The vertical axis represents the number of pixels that have that specific brightness value.

To display the histogram page, first take a picture. Press the ▣ button to switch on the LCD Monitor. The last recorded image will be shown. Now press ⊙ on the Multi-selector switch and scroll through the pages until the histogram is shown superimposed over the image.

***Assessing the Histogram:*** The shape and position of the histogram curve indicates the range of tones that have been captured in the picture. Dark tones will be distributed to the left of the histogram graph and light tones to the right. In a picture of a scene containing an average distribution of tones from dark shadow through mid-tones to bright highlights, the curve will start in the bottom left corner, slope upwards and then curve down to the bottom right corner. In this case a wide range of tones will have been recorded.

If the curve begins at a point some way up the left or right side of the histogram display, so the curve looks as though it has been cut off abruptly, the camera will not have recorded tones in either the shadows (left side) or highlights (right side), probably because the contrast level in the scene was beyond the capabilities of the camera. For example, an area of deep shadow in an otherwise brightly lit scene will hold no data and be recorded as solid black.

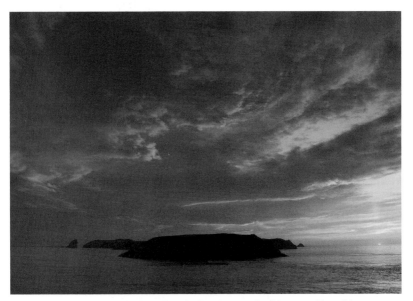

*Dark contrasty subjects often lack a range of mid tones. To achieve a successful image, the dark areas must be properly exposed with well-rendered bright areas to add drama and interest. To make sure you exposed the photo properly, check the LCD monitor's histogram.*

Generally, controlling exposure to retain highlight detail is more important than capturing perfect detail in shadow areas. If the histogram curve is weighted heavily toward the right side of the graph and is cut-off at a point along the right-hand vertical axis, highlight data will have been lost. In this case reduce the exposure until the right-hand end of the curve stops on the bottom axis before it reaches the vertical one. Conversely, if shadow detail is important, make sure the curve stops on the bottom axis before it reaches the left-hand vertical axis.

Obviously not all scenes contain an even distribution of tones, because they have a natural predominance of light or dark areas. In these cases the histogram curve will be biased to the right (light scenes) or the left (dark scenes). However, provided the histogram curve stops on the bottom axis, before it reaches either end of the graph, the image will retain the fullest possible range of highlight or shadow tones.

120

Scenes that are low in contrast will have a curve that appears as a rather narrow "spike", and ends short of either the left or right-hand end of the bottom axis. You have two

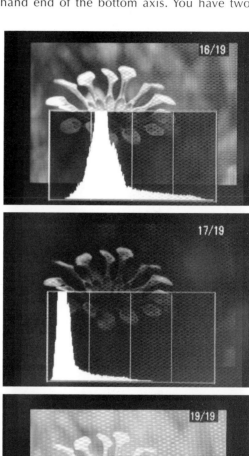

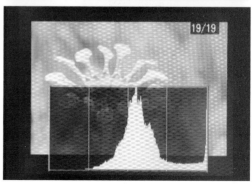

choices as to how to deal with this situation, either use the Tone Compensation function within the Custom option of the Optimizing Image control (see page 77 for further details) to have the contrast control performed by the camera, or adjust the contrast level at a later stage in an image processing application.

The three pictures shown opposite represent a range of exposures:

- Properly exposed (top), the left and right-hand ends of the curve stop on the bottom axis at or closely approaching either side of the graph, indicating that all tones have been recorded.

- 2-stops underexposed (middle), the curve is heavily biased with a large peak on the left side and no graph on the right. This indicates that virtually no light tones were recorded. In this case, noise is likely to be emphasized.

- 2-stops overexposed (bottom), the curve is biased to the right half of the graph, with no exposure of dark tones and an extra peak that cuts-off on the right axis, showing that highlight detail will be "blown out" (not recorded). Such areas will appear pure white in the picture.

***Highlights:*** Another of the information pages available when reviewing an image in the LCD Monitor is the Highlights function. This shows the location within the picture of pixels that have exceeded a threshold value by causing them to flash. If a significant area, or areas of the image flashes, you have probably overexposed the entire picture, and at the very least will have lost highlight detail. You will need to reduce exposure by setting a lower ISO value, a smaller (larger f/number) lens aperture, or a faster (shorter) shutter speed.

## Digital Infrared Photography

Black-and-white infrared pictures typically exhibit a course grain, with glowing white highlights and solid black shadows, particularly those shot on Kodak's HIE film. It is possible to emulate this effect with the D50.

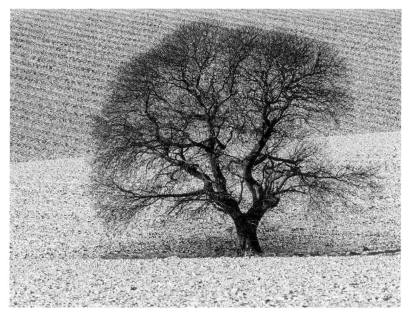

*Infrared photography records the end of the spectrum beyond the visible wavelengths of red and hence, a different world than what the eye can see. With film cameras special film must be loaded for this type of photography but the Nikon D50 makes it possible to shoot infrared photos anytime you want.*

Many digital cameras have the ability to record light beyond the limits of the spectrum visible to the human eye, particularly in the region of near Infrared (IR) around a wavelength of 780nm (one nanometer = one millionth of a millimeter). Camera designers work hard to exclude IR light from digital cameras, because it adversely affects apparent sharpness, reduces the contrast in skies, and can reveal unappealing features of skin that would otherwise not be visible.

***The D50 and IR:*** The filter array in front of the D50's CCD includes a filter designed to reduce the transmission of IR light; it is this filter that produces the green tint when you look at the CCD in the camera. Although Nikon has reduced the sensitivity of the D50 to IR, it is still capable of recording IR light. First, you will need an IR filter to exclude most if not all the visible spectrum. These are available with a variety of different "cut-off" points (the wave length below which they do not transmit light), from several manufacturers (see table on next page). You will need to mount the camera on a tripod due to the relatively long exposure times that will be required even in bright sunlight, because these filters are either semi-opaque, or totally opaque to visible light.

The most favorable time for IR photography is on a bright sunny day, because the level of IR light will be significantly higher compared with overcast conditions. To compensate for the fact that IR light is focused in a different plane than visible light, stop the lens down to a small aperture (f/11 or f/16). Set the white balance to Direct Sunlight, and switch to manual focusing. Mount the camera to a tripod, compose the shot and lock the tripod head. Then attach the IR filter.

**IR Filters:** Generally, it is best to use an IR filter with a low cut-off point, such as the Heliopan RG695 (695nm), or Kodak Wratten 89B (695nm), because they transmit sufficient visible light to allow the D50's exposure meter to function accurately. Although you will be able to see very little, if anything, through the viewfinder, adjust the shutter speed to obtain a "correct" exposure. Finally, release the shutter. The picture will have a strong red cast but this can be corrected at a later stage in an image processing application.

Using a darker IR filter such as a Kodak Wratten 87 (780nm) reduces the red cast but requires the exposure to be increased by anything up to three or four stops, since filters of this type remove virtually all the visible light. Consequently, you should not rely on the reading suggested by the D50's exposure meter. The D50 will even respond with a visually opaque filter such as a Kodak Wratten 87C (830nm), but exposures become impracticably long with a distinct risk of causing hot pixels.

**Hint:** For shutter speeds in excess of one second it is advisable to set the long exposure noise reduction option to ON in the Shooting Menu (Note: image processing times will increase by more than double). The default setting is OFF.

Here is a list of some of the IR filters that are available from various manufacturers:

## IR Filters

| Filter Designation | Wavelength Cut-off (nm) | Manufacturer |
|---|---|---|
| RG695 | 695 | Heliopan |
| 89B | 710 | Kodak |
| BW092 | 710 | B&W |
| IR72 | 720 | Hoya |
| RG780 | 780 | Heliopan |
| 87 | 780 | Kodak |
| 87C | 830 | Kodak |

*The green dots next to the* 🔳 *and* 🎛 *Buttons signify that you can press both simultaneously to return to the D50's default settings.*

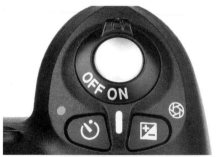

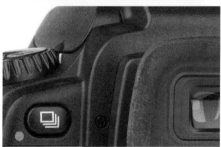

## Resetting Default Values

If you want to restore settings on the D50 to their default values, press and hold the ● and ◉ buttons. The green dots beside each button are a reminder of their function for this feature.

Using the two-button reset function of the D50 restores the default settings as shown in the tables below:

### Shooting Menu Settings

| Setting | Default Value |
|---|---|
| Optimize Image | Normal |
| Image Quality | JPEG Normal |
| Image Size | Large (3008 x 2000) |
| White balance | Auto |
| ISO (sensitivity) | 200 in P. S. A. M modes<br>200 in DVP modes if CS-9 is OFF |

### Custom Menu Settings

| Setting | Default Value |
|---|---|
| CS-6 (Flash level) | Off (0.0) |
| CS-12 (Bracketing Set) | Off |
| CS-13 (Metering) | Matrix |

### Other Camera Settings

| Setting | Default Value |
|---|---|
| Shooting Mode | Single |
| Focus area | Center |
| Focus lock | Off |
| Flexible Program | Off |
| Auto-exposure lock | Off |
| Exposure compensation | Off (0.0) |
| Flash sync mode | P, S, A, M – Front curtain fill-flash |
| | Auto, Portrait, Child,<br>Close-up – Auto front curtain |
| | Night-portrait – Auto Slow |

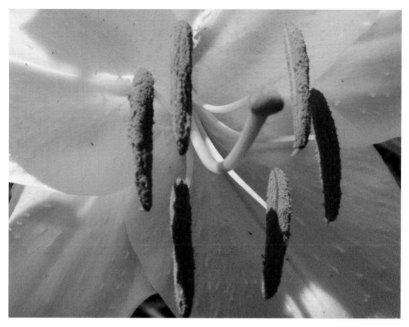

*Black and white often adds a dramatic touch to a photo and digital makes it easy to do. You can convert color photos to grayscale in most image processing programs. ©Kevin Kopp*

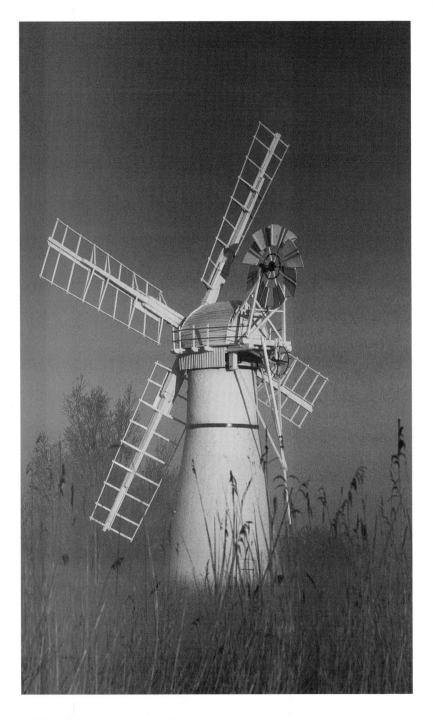

# Menus and Custom Settings

The D50 makes extensive use of its menu system, which is displayed on the LCD monitor. This is divided into four sections:

1) **Setup Menu**—This is used to establish the basic configuration of the camera.

2) **Shooting Menu**—This is used to select more sophisticated camera controls.

3) **Playback Menu**—This is used for managing the pictures stored on the memory card.

4) **Custom Settings Menu**—This is used to select and set specific controls, which fine-tune camera operations.

To access any menu, push the [MENU] button and press on the Multi Selector Switch to highlight one of the four tabs used to identify each menu: ⚙ Setup Menu, ▢ Shooting Menu, ▶ Playback Menu, and ✐ Custom Settings. Highlight the required menu tab by using the and then press to open it. You navigate to the specific option by using on the Multi Selector Switch.

*Note:* Both the Custom Setting and Setup menus can be displayed in either basic, or detailed forms. Whichever you choose use the multi-selector switch to scroll up or down through the options.

In those instances where controls within the menu system are duplicated by the use of buttons and dials located on the camera body, I would recommend using the latter option because this will reduce battery power consumption.

*Many of the D50's image controls are available in its Shooting menu including Image Quality, Image Size, and Long Exposure Noise Reduction.*

In this section I will deal with those features and functions controlled by the various menus that have not been discussed elsewhere in this book, and give page references to more detailed descriptions for the remainder.

## Setup Menu (Basic Form)

### Format
See page 41 for detailed information.

### CSM/Setup Menu
This option allows you to select either the Simple (short) or Detailed (full) lists of the options available in the Custom Settings and Setup menus.

### Date
See page 39 for detailed information.

### LCD Brightness
To adjust the brightness of the LCD Monitor, highlight LCD Brightness and press ⊙ on the multi-selector switch. This displays a grayscale and the current brightness setting. To adjust the brightness, press ⊙ on the multi selector switch, and confirm the setting by pressing ⊙ .

*Note:* Since visual assessment of the image for accuracy of exposure and color fidelity is unreliable on the LCD monitor due to the limitations of the screen it is probably best to leave this control set to its default value of 0.

### Video Mode
Use this mode to select the video standard that matches your video device (i.e., a television or VCR). You can select either NTSC or PAL.

### Language
See page 38 for detailed information.

## Image Comment

This option allows you to attach a brief (maximum 36-charater) comment to each image. Highlight Image comment and press ⊙ on the multi-selector switch. Then highlight Input comment and press ⊙ on the multi selector switch to open a page that displays a dialog box containing the character set, a comment field, and brief instructions. Use the multi selector switch to highlight the desired character and press ▣ to enter that character into the comment field. To move the cursor around the dialog box, press ▣ and rotate the Command dial; the cursor moves in the same direction as the dial. To delete a character at the current cursor position, press the ▣ button. Once you have composed the comment, press the ▣ button, which returns you to the image comment menu.

To attach the comment to all subsequent images, highlight Attach comment and press ⊙ on the multi selector switch. A checkmark will appear in the box next to Attach comment; then highlight Done and press ⊙ on the multi-selector switch to confirm the setting.

If you do not want the comment to be attached return to the Image comment menu, highlight Attach comment and uncheck the box by pressing ⊙ ; then highlight Done and press ⊙ on the multi selector switch to confirm the setting.

**Hint:** It would be very time consuming to change the comment on a regular basis; therefore you will probably want to settle on a universal comment that identifies the image as belonging to you, for example, Copyright Picture: Simon Stafford.

## USB

See page 203 for detailed information.

## Setup Menu (Detailed Form)

By selecting to display the Detailed form of the Setup menu the following additional options are available:

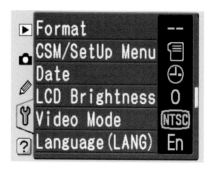

### Folders

The D50 uses a folder system to organize images stored on the camera's memory card; the default folder name is NCD50.

If you do not use any of the options pertaining to folders, the camera creates a folder named 100NCD50 (abbreviated to NCD50 in the menu) in which the first 999 pictures stored on the card will be placed. If you were to exceed 999 pictures, the D70 creates a new folder named 101NCD50, and so on for each set of 999 pictures.

You can create your own folder(s), although their name will always be pre-fixed by a three digital number assigned by the camera, and be limited to a five-character title. Open the Folder menu and highlight New and select it by pressing ; a dialog box containing the character set (0-9, and A-Z upper case only), a comment field, and brief instructions will be displayed. Use the same method as described under the Image Comment section above to create the folder name and press ENTER to confirm it.

If you use multiple folders, you must select one as the active folder. During shooting all images will be stored in this folder until either an alternative folder is chosen, or the maximum capacity of 999 pictures in the active folder capacity is exceeded, in which case the D50 will create a new folder using the same five-character suffix and assign a three-digit prefix with an incremental increase of one. For example, if you create a folder named 100SPORT and you shoot until it contains a maximum of 999 pictures, as soon as the next exposure is made the D50 creates a new folder called 101SPORT where pictures will be stored until it becomes full, or you select an alternative folder as the active folder.

*Note:* For the purposes of selecting images and naming folders the D50 deals with all folders with the same name (regardless of their prefix) as though they are a single folder. So, in the example above if you chose the folder named Sport all pictures in Sport (100Sport, and 101Sport) will be selected.

Folders can be renamed if you wish and empty folders can be deleted.

**Hint:** Folders may be useful if you expect to take pictures of a variety of subjects (i.e. you go away on a tour and want to file your images on the memory card location-by-location. You can create a folder for each location and select this as the active folder accordingly).

**Hint:** Personally, I find that using multiple folders is time consuming, potentially confusing, and fraught with danger! If you have more than one D-SLR camera and move cards between them, the individual cameras will not be able to handle images in folders created by another camera. If the second camera then creates a new folder, it will have a higher prefix number than the folder created by the first camera. Even multiple folders created by the D50 can present problems, as images will be saved to the currently selected folder with the highest prefix number. I prefer to use a browser application such as Picture Project, or Nikon View to organize my folders and image files.

## File Number Sequence

Using this option you can specify when the D50 resets file numbers. There are three alternatives:

**OFF**—At this default setting file numbers are always reset to 0001 whenever a new folder is created, when the memory card is formatted, or a new storage card is inserted in the camera.

**ON**—File numbers increase incrementally from the last number used until they reach 9999 whenever a new folder is created, when the memory card is formatted, or a new storage card is inserted in the camera. At this point a new folder is created and file numbering begins again from 0001.

**Reset**—Similar to ON, except the next image taken is assigned a file number by adding one to the highest file number in the current folder. If the selected folder contains no pictures the file numbering is reset to 0001.

To select the File Sequence Numbering, highlight the option in the Setup Menu and press ⌣ on the multi selector switch. Navigate to your chosen option and press ⌣ on the multi selector switch to select it.

## Mirror Lock-Up

See page 44 for detailed information.

## Dust Reference Photo

This feature is used to acquire a reference frame that can be applied in the Image Dust Off function available in Nikon Capture 4.3 or later. You must have a CPU lens attached to the camera (Nikon recommends using a focal length of 50mm of more).

Highlight Dust ref photo and press ⌣ on the multi-selector switch. This will display two options: Yes and No. If you want to cancel this function highlight No and press ⌣ on the multi-selector switch. To proceed highlight Yes and press ⌣ on the multi selector switch. A message will be displayed on the LCD monitor, Take photo of white object

10cm from lens, and *rEF* will appear in the control panel and viewfinder displays.

*Note:* If you decide you want to cancel the function at this stage and return to the Setup menu press the ⊞ button.

Point the lens at a brightly lit, featureless white test target approximately 4 inches (10 cm) from the camera, ensuring that no shadow is cast on the target area. Then press the shutter release button halfway (if the camera is set to perform autofocus the lens will shift to infinity automatically; in manual focus mode you must manually adjust the lens to the infinity focus position).

*Note:* Following this procedure produces a completely defocused image in the camera's viewfinder, which is intentional. Do not attempt to acquire a sharply focused image of the test target in the viewfinder.

Finally, depress the shutter release button fully to record the Image Dust Off reference information. If the exposure is successful the LCD monitor will display a checkerboard pattern and the file information will show a file name with a file extension of .NDF. It is not possible to view the Image Dust Off reference as an image either in the camera or on a computer.

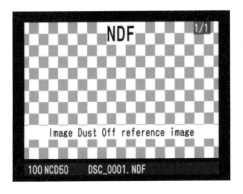

If the test target is too bright or too dark, and the D50 is unable to record the Image Dust Off reference information properly a warning message EXPOSURE SETTINGS NOT APPROPRIATE will be shown on the LCD Monitor. In this case, find an alternative target, and repeat the procedure.

**Hint:** The Dust Off Reference feature works well but it is neither foolproof, nor a substitute for keeping the filter array in front of the CCD sensor clean.

*Note:* When you shoot over a protracted period and cleaning the filter array is not practicable it may be necessary to make several reference files at different stages, because it is likely the position and number of any particles present will alter.

## Firmware Version

To check the current version of the firmware installed on your D50, highlight Firmware Ver. and press ⊙ on the multi-selector switch. To return to the Setup menu highlight Done and press ⊙ on the multi-selector switch.

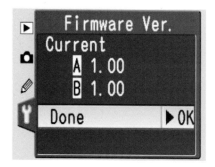

## Image Rotation

At its default setting of Automatic the D50 will record the orientation of the camera at the time of each exposure so that the images will be displayed in the correct orientation when reviewed on the camera, or opened within Nikon software. This option can be switched off, if desired, by highlighting Off and pressing (right arrow icon) on the multi-selector switch.

136

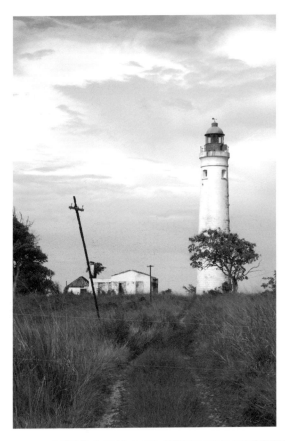

At its default setting, the D50 "remembers" the orientation of the camera and displays images on its LCD monitor with correct orientation when the camera is held in standard horizontal position for viewing. Thus the size of vertical or portrait format photos is reduced so that they can be viewed without rotating the camera. Because the upright vertical image is smaller, viewing is more difficult. In this case, you may prefer to disable this function by selecting the Off option.
©Mimi Netzel

**Hint:** To display a picture shot in the vertical (portrait) orientation on the LCD monitor of the D50 it must be reduced in size to fit the screen dimensions, which makes viewing it more difficult. Therefore you may wish to consider disabling this function by selecting the Off option. However, if you do this it will be necessary to rotate images manually to view them in the correct orientation when opened subsequently in Nikon software.

***Note:*** When taking pictures with the lens pointing up or down the D50 may not record the correct orientation. In this case select the Off option.

## Shooting Menu

Most of the Shooting Menu controls have been dealt with elsewhere; the relevant page numbers are given below as a reference.

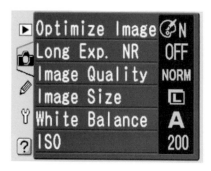

### Optimize Image
See page 77 for detailed information.

### Long Exposure Noise Reduction
Although the D50 processes all images with an automatic noise reduction feature, for exposures in excess of about one second a further control can be selected manually. In the Shooting menu highlight Long Exp. NR and highlight ON followed by pressing ⊙ on the multi selector switch to select it.

   After a picture has been taken, *Job nr* appears flashing, in both the control panel and viewfinder display, while the image data is being processed. During this time the shutter release is disabled. As soon as *Job nr* stops flashing the shutter release becomes active again.

*Note:* While the long exposure noise reduction feature is active the camera will take more than twice as long to process each image.

### Image Quality
See pages 70-73 for detailed information.

## Image Size
See pages 70-73 for detailed information.

## White Balance
Adjustments to the white balance value can only be made in Program, Aperture-Priority, Shutter-Priority, and Manual exposure modes (see pages 74-75 for detailed information).

## ISO (Sensitivity)
Adjustments to the sensitivity (ISO equivalent) can be made when the D50 is set to Program, Aperture-priority, Shutter-priority, or Manual exposure modes. In the DVP modes sensitivity can be adjusted provided CS-9 ISO Control is set to Off (see pages 99-102 for detailed information).

# Playback Menu

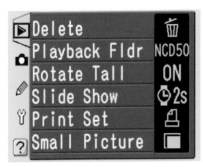

*Note:* There must be a memory card inserted in the camera for the Playback menu to be displayed.

It is possible to select multiple images in the Delete-Selected, Print Set-Selected, and Small Picture options within this menu. Open the required option, highlight the appropriate image with the yellow border box by pressing  ☺ , and press the  ☺ ◄ to select it (a small icon will appear within the yellow border box as a confirmation). If you wish to deselect a particular image highlight it with the yellow border box and press the ☺  and ensure the warning icon is no longer displayed.

## Delete Images

This option allows you to delete either a selected group of images or all images, which is much quicker than deleting images individually. Highlight Delete in the Playback Menu and press ⊙ to select it. You have the option of deleting a selected set of images or deleting all the images in the selected folders in the Playback folder menu.

If you choose to select individual pictures, highlight Selected and up to six images will be displayed on the LCD Monitor. A yellow border box will surround one picture to highlight it. Use ⊙ to scroll through the images, and ⊙ to mark an image for deletion. Repeat this process for each image until all the required images are marked. Press the ⬛ button and a page will appear showing the total number of images to be deleted, together with a Yes/No option to confirm the delete command. You will see this same page displayed with the same Yes/No option to confirm the delete command, if you select the All option from the Delete page menu.

## Playback Folder

You can choose to have only those images in the current folder available for playback, or alternatively select images in all folders to be available.

Highlight Playback fldr in the Playback Menu and press ⊙ to select it. This will display a page with two options: Current and All. Highlight your chosen option and press ⊙ to select it. Current will display images in the folder currently selected for image storage. All will allow you to playback images in all folders created by cameras that comply with the Design Rule for Camera File System (DCF), which includes all Nikon digital cameras.

*The Playback menu's slide show option allows you to view your pictures and share them with others. During this type of playback you can pause, and go forward or backward. ©Mimi Netzel*  ⇨

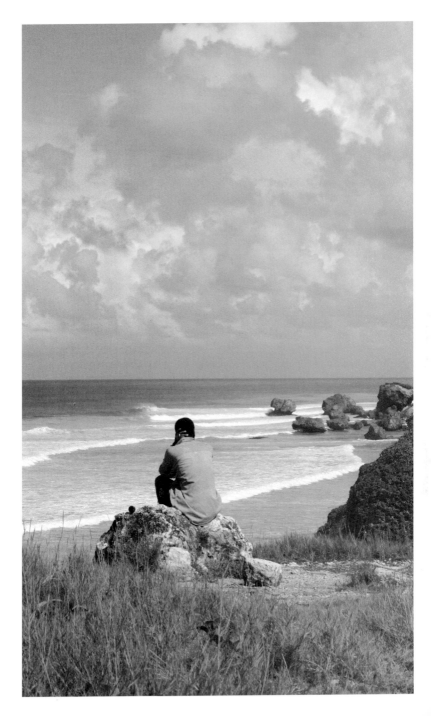

*Note:* If you have multiple folders with the same name differentiated only by the three-digit prefix and select Current all pictures in these folders will be played back.

## Rotate Tall

This option works in conjunction with the Image Rotation option in the Setup menu. To display pictures in the Playback menu that were taken in the vertical (portrait) format select the Yes option from the Rotate Tall menu. Highlight Rotate tall and press ⊙ to select it. Highlight either Yes or No, and press ⊙ to set the option. Any pictures taken with Off selected for Image Rotation will be displayed in the horizontal (landscape) format.

**Hint:** Due to the dimensions of the LCD Monitor, and the 3:2 aspect ratio of the full frame area, a picture displayed in the vertical orientation will be two-thirds the size of one displayed in the horizontal orientation. Therefore, you may prefer to use the auto-rotate command within Picture Project or Nikon View to perform this action once you have imported the images into your computer.

## Slide Show

Images stored on the memory card can be displayed automatically in sequence for a user-defined duration. Highlight Slide show in the menu and press ⊙ to select the option. This opens a page with two further options: Start and Frame intvl. Selecting Start begins a slide show of all images in the folder selected in the Playback Fldr menu. Pictures are shown in the order in which they were recorded, with a short pause between them. During the course of the slide show a number of operations can be performed. Use the ⊙⊙ to shift to the previous or next frame, the ⊙ to view shooting information, press ⊞ to pause the slide show, press the ⊞ to exit the slide show and return to the Playback menu, press ⊡ to exit the side show and return to playback mode, or press the shutter release button half way to end the slide show and return to the shooting mode.

142

After the last image has been displayed, or the ⬛ button is pressed to pause the playback, a dialog box appears in the LCD Monitor showing two further options; press ⊙ on the multi selector switch to select Restart or Frame Intvl. To exit the slide show and return to the Playback menu highlight Exit, and press ⊙ on the multi-selector switch, or press the ⬛ button.

To adjust the duration of display for each image, select Frame Intvl and scroll to the required time (2, 3, 5, or 10 seconds) to highlight it, and then press ⊙ to select the desired time.

**Print Set**
See page 206 for detailed information.

**Small Picture**
Using this option the D50 can create low-resolution copies of selected pictures suitable for attaching to an e-mail message, or publishing on a web page. The menu is a little misleading because opening it highlights the Select Picture option but you need to select the image resolution first from the Choose Size option. So, open this option and confirm the file size you require from one of three alternatives: 640 x 480, 320 x 240, or 160 x 120 pixels. Once you have set the file size press (right arrow icon) to return to the main menu page and Select Pictures will be highlighted. Use the method described above to select either a single, or multiple images.

*Note:* Although small in size any additional picture created using this option will take up make storage space on the memory card in the camera, and when reviewed on either the camera or a computer will show a sequential file number to images already stored on the memory card. An image created with the Small Picture option is denoted by the file name prefix SSC and a file extension of .jpg.

# Custom Settings

Many of the default settings for the various functions and features of the D50 can be superseded or altered. This is achieved by using a menu of Custom Settings (CS), but you will need to scroll through the list of 21 options (20 numbered settings plus one for reset) each time you want to make an adjustment for a particular shooting situation, because unlike other Nikon D-SLR cameras, the D50 does not offer an option to memorize a series of settings.

## Simple Menu

In an effort to simplify and speed-up this process, Nikon saw fit to offer two different levels of Custom Setting menus. The default menu only shows the first six options from the entire list of 20 plus the reset option. However, I find Nikon's idea of the six most useful options is somewhat curious, because I consider items such as the bracketing set and self-timer delay to be more important than, say, the audible warning and the option to operate the camera with no memory card installed.

## Detailed Menu

To work with to the full list, select the Setup Menu tab and scroll to CSM Menu. Press the multi-selector switch to the right and highlight Detailed, then select it by pressing the multi-selector switch to the right again.

Both Simple and Detailed menus, plus all Custom Settings, are selected using the same method. To view the selected menu, press the Menu button and, using the multi-selector switch, highlight the Custom Setting tab. Click the multi-selector switch to the right again and then use either the ⊙ , or turn the Command Dial to scroll through the menu. If you see a Custom Setting that is grayed out in the menu it indicates that it is not available. This may occur for a number of reasons including the exposure mode that is selected, and whether the lens is set for manual or automatic focusing.

*Note:* Both menus wrap-around in a continuous loop in both directions as you scroll (just keep pressing either the up or down arrow on the multi-selector switch, or turning the command dial).

Once you have selected a particular Custom Setting, click the multi-selector switch to the right use to view the sub-options. Highlight the desired sub-option by using either the up or down arrow on the multi-selector switch, and click the multi-selector switch to the right in order to confirm it (OK).

**Help Button**

To save you from carrying and referring to the instruction manual every time you want to know what a particular Custom Setting does, Nikon has provided a help-function that displays a brief description of each setting on the LCD Monitor. Whenever you have a Custom Setting displayed on the monitor, just press and hold the ⬛ button located on the camera back to the left of the monitor.

**Menu Reset**

All 20 numbered options within the Custom Setting menu have a default value. If, at anytime, you wish to cancel all your user-set Custom Settings and restore the camera to its default values, you should select CS-R (Menu Reset) and highlight Reset and press the multi-selector switch to the right to confirm (OK).

*Note:* This option only resets the Custom Setting menu it does not restore defaults in other camera menus.

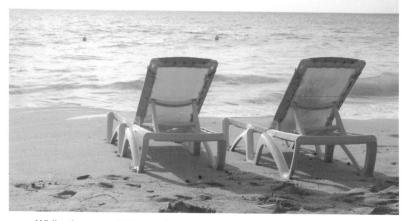

*While the new AF-A mode is the D50's default autofocus mode, I prefer to useCS-2 to select single-servo AF (AF-S). I prefer this because the camera will not fire until it has found focus in AF-S mode. ©Mimi Netzel*

## The Custom Settings List

### CS-1 Beep:

*Operation:* The D50 emits an audible, electronic beep when it has performed certain functions: during self-timer operation; when focus has been acquired in single-servo AF (AF-S); and an exposure is made remotely in quick-response mode using the ML-L3 remote control.

*Options:* **ON**—(default) the Control Panel shows (icon for Beep warning)
**OFF**—the Control Panel shows (icon for Beep cancelled) and the warning tone is cancelled

*Suggestion:* Set this option to OFF because the beep can be a distraction in many shooting situations.

**CS-2 Autofocus:**

*Operation:* The D50 has three different autofocus modes: automatic Autofocus (AF-A), single-servo autofocus (AF-S), and continuous-servo autofocus (AF-C). If either of the two latter modes is selected AF-S and AF-C are displayed in the control panel to indicate the active mode. If you chose the default option of AF-A no icon is shown in the control panel.

*Options:* **AF-A**—(default) the camera selects either AF-S, or AF-C, automatically depending on the shooting autofocus mode selection
**AF-S**—single-servo AF
**AF-C**—continuous-servo AF

*Suggestion:* The AF-A mode available on the D50 is a new innovation for a Nikon D-SLR camera; personally I have reservations about how useful it is, since at the time of the exposure you do not know which autofocus mode the camera is using. To ensure the camera has acquired focus before the shutter is released, you will want to use AF-S, so leave this option set to the default. The exception is when you are shooting fast action or sport when AF-C is probably more useful (see pages 93-94 for more information on focusing modes).

**CS-3 AF-Area Mode:**

*Operation:* The D50 has three different autofocus area modes, which determine how the autofocus operates.

*Options:* **Single Area**—the user selects one of the five focus areas manually and only this area is used to acquire focus (default for P, S, A, M and Close-Up Digital Vari-Program exposure modes).
**Dynamic Area**—the user selects a single focus area but the D50 uses information from the

147

other four AF areas to monitor the subject and if it determines the subject is outside the selected area it will shift focusing accordingly (default for the Sports Digital Vari-Program exposure mode).

**Closest subject**—the camera selects, automatically, the AF area with the subject deemed to be closest to the camera (default for the AUTO, Portrait, Landscape, Child, and Night Portrait Digital Vari-Programs).

*Suggestion:* The default setting is probably the safest bet for most situations in each of the exposure modes since it is the most predictable method of using autofocus.

When shooting a moving subject that shifts erratically, dynamic area is most useful because it tracks the subject by switching from the sensor area that is selected initially to the next most appropriate area according to the movement of the subject and the predictions of the camera's AF system.

Closest subject priority can be fooled easily if something suddenly moves in front of your main subject just as you are about to shoot, and the camera will re-focus rendering the intended subject out-of-focus, so take care!

**CS-4 No SD Card?:**

*Operation:* To prevent the D50 from appearing as though it is recording pictures when in fact it is not tat the default setting of this function the shutter release button is disabled when the camera does not contain a memory card. This control can be overridden to allow the camera to save pictures directly to a computer using Nikon Capture software.

*Options:* **Release lock**—(default) the shutter will not operate if no memory card is installed.

**Enable release**—the shutter release will operate normally even with no memory card
installed in the D50, and an image will be displayed on the LCD monitor but it will not be
saved in the camera.

*Suggestion:* Leave this option set to the default—Release
lock otherwise the D50 will appear to be operating normally but no pictures will be
recorded!

## CS-5 Image Review:

*Operation:* The D50 is capable of displaying an image in the
LCD Monitor after an exposure has been made.

*Options:* **ON**—(default) pictures are automatically shown
on the LCD Monitor immediately after an expo-
sure is made.
**OFF**—pictures are not displayed on the LCD
Monitor after an exposure unless the Playback
Button is pressed.

*Suggestion:* Unless you are very concerned about conserv-
ing battery power, in which case set this option
to OFF, it is generally useful to have the picture
displayed to confirm an exposure has been
made and to assess its quality using either the
histogram or highlight warning screens. As soon
as you have finished looking at the picture you
can switch the monitor off by lightly pressing
the shutter release button.

## CS-6 Flash Level:

*Operation:* The output of the built-in, or an external Speedlight flash unit attached to the D50, can be
adjusted via this option but it is only available
in P, A, S, and M exposure modes.

*Options:* The level of compensation can be adjusted over a range of +1EV to –3EV in increments of either 0.3EV or 0.5EV depending on which value is set at CS-11.

*Suggestion:* You will probably want to use this option if you use the built-in Speedlight for daylight fill-flash, which will require setting a minus compensation factor to reduce the influence of the flash on the overall exposure (see page 168 for further details). However, a far quicker and more convenient way to set flash compensation is to press and hold the **❹** + **🅑** **🔂** while turning the command dial.

**CS-7 AF Assist:**

*Operation:* The AF-assist Lamp, employed to aid the autofocus system, lights automatically when the D50 determines that light levels are low and there is a risk that the AF system will not be able to acquire focus. However, the lamp has a maximum effective range of only 9' 10" (3m), and there are all sorts of limitations depending on the type of lens in use,

*Options:* **ON**—(default) AF-assist Lamp functions automatically.
**OFF**—the AF-assist Lamp will not operate regardless of the ambient light level.

*Suggestion:* This is very much a personal opinion, but I keep the lamp switched off, as it is either a potential distraction to the subject, or of questionable value due to its limited operating range.

## CS-8 AF Area Illum

*Operation:* To assist in identifying which AF sensor is active, particularly in difficult lighting conditions, the D50 can be set to highlight the focusing screen markings briefly in red with the relevant set of brackets shown as a solid line whilst the other four non-active sensors and the central 8mm circle only show as a fainter outline.

*Options:* **Auto**—highlighting will only occur if the camera determines the need to do so according to the level of contrast between the subject and background.
**Off**—this function is disabled regardless of lighting conditions.
**On**—this function always operates regardless of lighting conditions.

*Suggestion:* Choice will depend on your own personal preference. I know some users feel the highlight function can a distraction whilst others find it indispensable.

## CS-9 ISO Control:

*Operation:* In line with the ability of the D50 to be used in a totally automated way the camera can be set to adjust its sensitivity (equivalent to a film's ISO rating) automatically when used in one of the seven Digital Vari-Program (DVP) modes. So, regardless of the prevailing light level the camera chooses a combination of shutter speed and lens aperture biased appropriately for the selected DVP mode. ISO Auto is displayed in both the viewfinder and control panel as a reminder.

*Options:* **ON**—(default) in the Digital Vari-Program modes only the D50 sets the sensitivity level automatically according to the shooting conditions.

**OFF**—the ISO Control function is disabled and the sensitivity setting selected via the Set Up menu will be used by the camera during exposure calculations in the DVP modes.

*Suggestion:* If you are content to use your D50 in a completely automated 'point and shoot' way you may as well leave this option at its default setting. However, I would recommend selecting OFF and selecting the lowest possible sensitivity level for the shooting conditions to ensure maximum image quality.

**CS-10 ISO Auto:**

*Operation:* The D50 automatically adjusts its sensitivity (equivalent to a film's ISO rating) to a higher level if it cannot achieve an appropriate combination of shutter speed and lens aperture for the prevailing light level and selected exposure mode. This function operates with all of the exposure modes available on the D50 (P, A, S, M, and DVP).

*Options:* **OFF**—(default) the ISO Auto function is disabled and the camera retains the sensitivity setting (ISO equivalent) you select regardless of the exposure settings.
**ON**—it will raise the sensitivity setting (ISO equivalent) automatically with in the range of ISO200 and 1600. The camera displays ISO AUTO in the control panel and the viewfinder display when this option is selected, and the ISO Auto icon flashes as a warning that the camera has altered the ISO setting selected by the user. However, there is no indication as to what ISO setting is in use!

*Suggestion:* Leave this function set to the default—Off—if you want to be sure of what the camera is doing. I have seen several photographers perplexed by this Custom Setting, as they failed to understand why their exposures had altered, because they had not realized it had been active.

If you do want to use this function in P, A, and DVP modes I recommend you set a shutter speed no longer than the default setting of 1/30 second to reduce the risk of camera shake. Choose the shutter speed you want, press the multi-selector switch to the right, and select Done to set the value.

*Note:* The Nikon instruction book is rather ambiguous on this option with its reference to "a maximum" shutter speed that the user can set in P, A, and the DVP exposure modes. This is probably due to the translation from Japanese to English; I believe the word "longest" would be more appropriate. In these exposure modes if the shutter speed selected by the camera is greater than your "longest" chosen shutter speed, the camera will increase the sensitivity accordingly.

## CS-11 EV Step:

*Operation:* This determines the size of the increment for adjustments pertaining to exposure (shutter speed & lens aperture), exposure compensation, flash output compensation, and bracketing. This can be set to shift in one of two increments, which is then used for all exposure settings on the D50.

*Options:* **1/3 Step**—the D50 makes adjustments in increments of 1/3-EV (1/3-stop) (default).
**1/2 Step**—the D50 makes adjustments in increments of 1/2-EV (1/2-stop)

*Suggestion:* Leave the D50 at the default option to give you the finest level of control over exposure.

## CS-12 BKT Set:

*Operation:* This option allows you to choose the routine the D50 uses to perform exposure bracketing.

*Options:* **Off**—this is the default setting and no bracketing of either exposure or white balance is performed.

**AE & flash**—this option adjusts the shutter speed/aperture values for the ambient exposure AND the flash exposure level. A sub-menu allows you to select the level of +/- compensation applied, which can be done in increments of either 0.3EV, or 0.5EV depending on the option selected at CS-11 up to a maximum of +/-2EV. Each bracketing series is comprised of three exposures; the first without adjustment, the second underexposed by the chosen increment, and the third overexposed by the same amount. In continuous shooting mode the camera will stop after each three-exposure bracket sequence.

**WB bracketing**—white balance values are bracketed for JPEG files only, and no exposure bracketing takes place. This option is not available for NEF, or NEF+JPEG file options. You will need to select the size of the increment by highlighting what Nikon refers to as a Step value of 1, 2, or 3. After each exposure the camera processes the image data to produce three separate pictures, the first is un-modified; the second is warmer (more red), and the third cooler (more blue).

*Note:* See pages 74-75 for more details of the white balance values used by the D50.

*Suggestion:* Since changing exposure by varying the shutter speed or aperture produces a very different appearance compared with changing the flash exposure level, you need to think carefully about this feature if you are using a Speedlight for fill-flash work, as the flash output will alter between each exposure in the bracketing set. Nikon provides no information about what each Step (increment) represents in terms of color temperature or MIRED (Micro Reciprocal Degree a method of calculating color temperature) value. In short, each increment is equivalent to a +/- 10-MIRED shift. So, selecting the 1 Step option is equivalent to using an 81 (pale red/amber) filter for the warmer version and an 82 (pale blue) filter for the cooler version. Likewise the 2 Step option is equivalent to the stronger effect of 81A and 82A filters, and the 3 Step option represents a greater color shift equivalent to 81B and 82B filters respectively.

## CS-13 Metering:

*Operation:* This option allows you to select the type of TTL metering the D50 performs in P, S, A, and M exposure modes.

*Options:* **Matrix**—the D50 uses a 480-segment Red-Green-Blue (RGB) sensor to assess exposure based on color, contrast and overall scene brightness. If the lens in use is a D or G-type the focus distance is also taken into consideration.

**Center-weighted**—although the metering system assesses the entire frame area it places a bias of 75% on the area defined by the 8mm diameter circle marked on the focusing screen.

*Note:* The specification printed in the first edition of the Nikon instruction manual suggests that the center-weighted metering pattern of the D50 can be selected from a 6, 8, 10, or 12mm diameter circle. This is incorrect the metering area is fixed at 8mm diameter.

**Spot**—the D50 meters from a 3.5mm (this represents approximately 2.3% of total frame area) diameter circle centered on the active focus brackets, which allows you to take a reading from a very precise section of the scene. This can be of great assistance, for example, if the background is particularly bright or dark and it would otherwise influence overall exposure assessment adversely.

*Suggestion:* For a majority of shooting situations I would recommend using the Matrix option. If you use a G- or D-type Nikkor lens this provides 3D Color Matrix metering in which the focus distance is taken into consideration when the D50 calculates an exposure value. Using either non-D AF or Ai P-type Nikkor lenses the metering defaults to Color Matrix metering.

*Note:* TTL metering will only function with a non-D AF, D-type AF, G-type AF, or Ai P-type manual focus lens attached to the D50. If you mount any other type of Nikkor lens on the D50 the metering system will not operate

## CS-14 AE-L/AF-L:

*Operation:* The auto-exposure lock (AE-L/AF-L) button can be assigned one of a variety of functions using this Custom Setting:

*Options:* **AE/AF Lock**—Exposure settings and autofocus are locked when the button is pressed and held down (default).
**AE Lock only**—Exposure is locked but autofocus continues to operate when the button is pressed and held down.
**AF Lock only**—Autofocus is locked but exposure values continue to shift when the button is pressed and held down.
**AE Lock hold**—Exposure is locked when the button is pressed and remains locked until it is pressed again.

**AF-ON**—Camera will only autofocus when the button is pressed; pressing the shutter release button will not activate autofocus.

**FV Lock**—Pressing the AE-L/AF-L button fires the monitor pre-flash sequence (no exposure is made) to calculate the required flash output. This value is then locked (insert FV lock icon is displayed in the viewfinder as a reminder) until the AE-L/AF-L button is pressed again, the TTL meter turns off automatically, or you switch the camera off.

*Note:* When the exposure is made, no pre-flash sequence operates.

*Suggestion:* AF Lock only can be useful when you know where the subject is going to be but want auto-exposure to operate right up to the moment you make the exposure.

AE Lock only is probably the most useful option as you can take a reading from your chosen area, lock it, and then recompose the shot before releasing the shutter.

AF-ON has two distinct ways of being used:

First, it can be considered as an extension of the AF lock feature. Pressing the button (ensure CS-2 is set to single-servo AF mode) operates AF using the active AF sensor without having to press the shutter release button. If you continue to hold the button down, you can recompose the shot before releasing the shutter as many times as you wish.

Second, it can be used to release the shutter when the subject reaches a pre-focused distance. Set the D50 to Single-servo/Single-area AF Modes and select AF-ON. Set the lens to Autofocus Mode and select an appropriate AF sensor area for your shot. Pre-focus by selecting a point through which the subject will move, align this with the AF sensor area bracket then press and release the AE-L button. Recompose the shot and press and hold the shutter release button down all the way (remember focus is now locked). The shutter will be released as soon as the selected AF sensor area bracket detects an in-focus subject. For example, say you are photographing a hurdle race, you pre-focus on the bar of a hurdle and then recompose so the AF bracket covers an area just above the bar where the athlete will pass through. As the runner approaches the hurdle, press and hold the shutter release down, while keeping the active AF bracket centered on the subject. As soon as the D50 detects the hurdler is in focus the shutter operates.

FV Lock is useful since monitor pre-flashes are not emitted when you press the Shutter Release Button, making it possible to trigger non-dedicated wireless slave cells in conjunction with the D50's shutter operation (the pre-flashes would otherwise trigger the slave cells prematurely). Use the settings available under CS-18 Meter-off to retain the FV Lock function for an appropriate period if you use the built-in flash for this purpose.

**CS-15 AE Lock:**

*Operation:* Many cameras lock auto-exposure when their shutter release button is depressed half way and held in that position. However, at its default setting the D50 does not.

*Options:* **AE-L Button**—the exposure is only locked when you press and hold the AE-L button (default).
**+ Release bttn**—the exposure can be locked by pressing and holding either the shutter release button halfway, or the AE-L button.

*Suggestion:* To my mind it is simpler and quicker to have the auto-exposure value locked by pressing and holding the shutter release button, so set + Release bttn

**CS-16 Flash Mode:**

*Operation:* This option sets the flash mode for the built-in Speedlight. It does not affect external Speedlight units.

*Options:* TTL The built-in flash operates in the i-TTL Mode and emits pre-flashes to determine required flash output automatically (default).
Manual Available in P, S, A, and M exposure modes only the flash output is fixed at a predetermined level selected from the sub-menu.

*Suggestion:* For most shooting situations the default TTL setting is probably the best option. If you do need a precise output from the built-in Speedlight select manual and use the Guide Number to calculate the appropriate lens aperture (see page 168).

**CS-17 Monitor Off: (Duration of LCD Monitor Display)**

*Operation:* This option sets the duration of the display on the LCD monitor from the time of the last associated action (e.g. pressing the (icon 95) button). This assumes no other function that would otherwise turn it off is activated subsequently. The duration can be chosen from the following times:

*Options:* 10s (ten seconds), 20s (twenty seconds— default), 1 min (one minute), 5 min (five minutes), and 10 min (ten minutes)
If you connect the D50 to an external power source such as the EH-5 AC adapter, the duration is automatically set to 10 minutes, which cannot be altered.

*Suggestion:* The LCD Monitor consumes a relatively high level of power, which you may wish to conserve by selecting a shorter duration than the default 20 seconds.

*Note:* The display can always be switched off by depressing the shutter release half way.

## CS-18 Meter-Off: (Duration of TTL Exposure Meter Function):

*Operation:* At the default setting the camera's meter remains active for 8-seconds after you depress the shutter release button half way and then release it, or you make an exposure. The duration of the metering display can be changed to the following values:

*Options:* 4s (four-seconds), 8s (eight-seconds—default), 16s (sixteen-seconds), and 30 min (thirty-minutes) If you connect the D50 to an external power source such as the EH-5 AC adapter, the duration is automatically set to 10 minutes, which cannot be altered.

*Suggestion:* The eight-second duration is generally long enough to view exposure data; any longer and the cumulative effect on battery power drain may be significant during the course of a day's shooting.

## CS-19 Self-Timer:

*Operation:* You can select one of four different durations for the delay between pressing the shutter release button and the exposure being made via the self-timer function as follows:

*Options:* 2s (two-seconds), 5s (five-seconds), 10s (default) (ten-seconds), and 20s (twenty-seconds)

*Suggestion:* The two-second delay is ideal for releasing the shutter when you want to minimize camera vibration caused by touching it but you need to re-set the self-timer function for each exposure. Therefore, the ML-L3 IR remote release is a more practical option.

**CS-20 Remote:**

*Operation:* This option allows you to determine the duration of the period in which the D50 can receive the IR signal from the ML-L3 remote control before it cancels the remote release function, automatically. The following delays are available:

*Options:* 1 min (default) (one-minute), 5 min (five-minutes), 10 min (ten-minutes), and 15 min (fifteen-minutes)

*Suggestion:* The camera is drawing more power than usual when it remains active awaiting the IR signal. Therefore, set the shortest duration according to the shooting conditions.

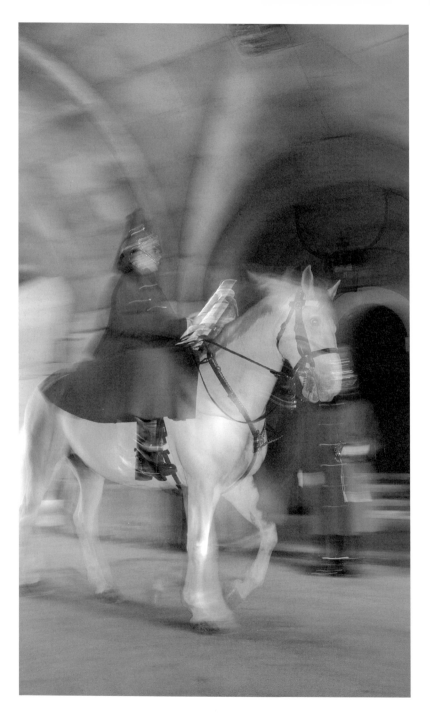

# Nikon Flash Photography

Flash is a highly useful tool in photography—not only for augmenting low-light levels but also for controlling contrast and applying creative lighting. Before we take a look at the flash capabilities of the D50, it is important to understand a basic principle of light called the Inverse Square Law, which has a direct bearing on flash photography. Put simply it states that if you double the distance from the light source (the flash) the light intensity is reduced by a factor of four. This is because light spreads out as it travels. So, at double the distance the light covers an area four times larger than at the original range. Since a flash unit emits a precise level of light, it will only light the subject correctly at a specific distance. If the flash exposes the subject correctly, then anything closer to the flash and lit by it solely will be overexposed, and consequently anything farther away from the subject will be increasingly underexposed. So, to produce a balanced exposure between the subject and its surroundings, you need to balance the light from the flash with the ambient (available or existing) light.

In order to accomplish this, the D50 meters flash using a 420-pixel sensor located in its viewfinder head. It then considers both the flash and ambient light levels in the final exposure computation. The D50 uses Nikon's third generation of TTL flash control; a system called i-TTL (Intelligent TTL). It is part of a wider set of flash functions that Nikon refers to as its Creative Lighting System (CLS).

*Nikon's Creative Lighting System offers the ability to use sophisticated flash techniques with your D50 camera. Here slow sync mode was used with an SB-800 Speedlight flash to create this intriguing photo of a horse in action.*

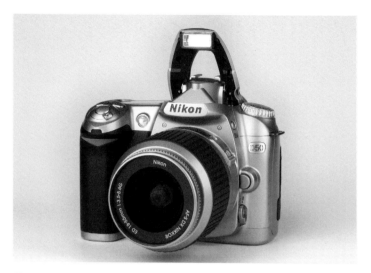

*The D50's built-in Speedlight comes in handy when a little extra light is needed either for adequate exposure or to fill-in shadows on a bright summer day.*

**Note:** Currently the internal Speedlights of the D50, D70, D70s, and the two external Speedlights, the SB-600 and SB-800, are the only Nikon flash units to support CLS. So if you have an earlier external Speedlight, including a DX-type, you will not have access to TTL flash control with the D50.

## Built-In Speedlight

The D50 features a built-in Speedlight (Nikon's proprietary name for its flash units) that has a guide number of 49 feet (15m) [56 feet (17m) in manual flash] at a sensitivity of ISO 200 equivalent and a lens focal length of 35mm. It can synchronize with the shutter at speeds up to 1/500th second. It has a minimum shooting distance of 2 feet (0.6 m) below that the camera will not necessarily calculate a correct flash exposure. Apart from the Auto, Portrait, Child, Close-up, and Night Portrait Digital Vari-Program modes that activate the flash automatically if it is required, the built-in Speedlight must be user activated by pressing the ⚡ button.

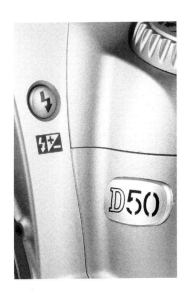

*The Flash Lock Release and Flash Mode button.*

The Speedlight draws its power from the camera's main battery; so extended use of the flash will have a direct effect on battery life. As soon as the flash unit pops up, it begins to charge. The ⚡ symbol appears in the viewfinder to indicate charging is complete and the flash is ready to fire. If the flash fires at its maximum output, the same ⚡ indicator will flash for approximately three seconds after the exposure has been made, as a warning of potential under-exposure.

*Note:* The flash-ready symbol ⚡ operates in the same way when an external Speedlight is attached to the D50.

**Flash Modes**
The D50's built-in Speedlight has two flash modes: TTL and Manual. These are set via Custom Setting-16 but Manual flash is only available when shooting in the P, A, S, or M exposure modes.

*i-TTL Balanced Fill-Flash Mode:* This is the default setting of the D50 with both the built-in and external SB-800 and SB-600 Speedlights. This mode requires a lens fitted with what Nikon refer to as a CPU (strictly speaking these lenses do

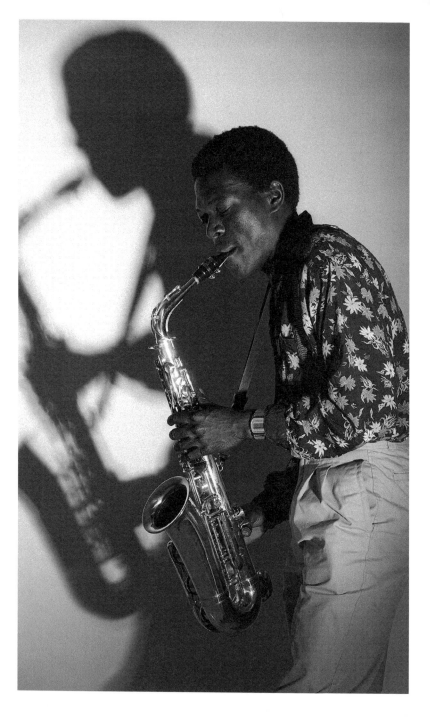

not have a CPU but a chip that communicates data to the camera body), so compatibility is available with the following Nikkor lens types: AI-P, AF, AF-D, AF-I, AF-S, and AF-G (all DX-Nikkor lenses are AF-G types).

*Note:* If you select Manual exposure mode or Spot metering the flash system defaults to standard TTL flash exposure control (see below).

The D50 calculates the ambient light and the flash exposure, using information from the Matrix metering system (including overall scene brightness and contrast range), lens data (focal length, focus distance, and aperture), and combines this with its assessment of a pair of low-intensity light pulses (something Nikon calls monitor pre-flashes) that are emitted rapidly immediately before the main flash discharge. The camera then attempts to produce a balanced exposure with a slight bias toward the ambient light component.

*Note:* Due to the low-intensity of the light output the preflash system of the built-in Speedlight is only effective up to a maximum distance of about 25 feet (6 m).

*Note:* In normal front-curtain sync the pre-flashes, which are emitted immediately before the reflex mirror lifts, and the main flash that occurs as soon as the shutter has opened, are perceived as a single flash of light. However, the pre-flashes can induce the blink reflex with some sensitive people, particularly children, so always check your pictures in the camera's lcd monitor.

Since all assessment of the flash output is performed before the shutter opens, if conditions change in that split second after the pre-flashes are fired, the flash exposure may be incorrect. With the D50 there is no TTL-flash control during the actual exposure as is the case with some Nikon film cameras.

*Don't underestimate the power of electronic flash in creative photography. Here the shadow from the use of indirect flash is exaggerated intentionally for its dramatic effect.*

***Standard TTL Flash Mode:*** The D50 automatically switches to this mode when it is set to M (Manual exposure) mode or when Spot metering is selected in P, A, and S modes. In Standard TTL mode, the camera attempts to calculate the flash output that will expose the subject correctly. It bases its assumptions on focus information (where the subject is located within the frame) and does not take into account the nature of the light, flash or ambient, from other areas of the scene (i.e. the foreground or background) as seen by the 420-pixel sensor.

**Hint:** Standard TTL is the best option if you want to shoot pictures with fill flash. In this mode any flash compensation you set will be applied to the exposure, unlike the automated i-TTL Balanced Fill-Flash mode, which will most probably override any setting you make and apply an unknown amount of flash compensation.

***Manual Flash Mode:*** In this mode the output of the Speedlight is fixed. It is necessary to calculate the correct lens aperture as determined by the flash-to-subject distance and the guide number (GN) of the Speedlight.

At its base sensitivity of ISO 200 (equivalent), the D50's built-in Speedlight has the following GN values:

| Power | GN (ft) | GN (m) |
|-------|---------|--------|
| Full  | 56      | 17     |
| 1/2   | 39      | 12     |
| 1/4   | 28      | 8.5    |
| 1/8   | 20      | 62     |
| 1/16  | 14      | 4.25   |

**Aperture = GN / Distance**

So, for example, with the D50's Speedlight set to 1/4-power, at a shooting distance of exactly 7 feet (3m), the lens aperture for a correct exposure of the subject will be f/4   (4 = 28/7).

168

*The D50's built-in Speedlight pops up automatically when needed in Full AUTO mode.*

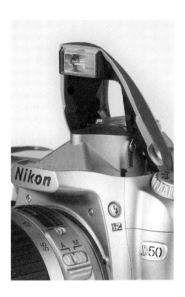

## Flash Sync Modes

These apply to the built-in Speedlight and the two external Speedlights, the SB-600 and SB-800. They determine when the flash is fired and how it interacts with the shutter. The flash sync modes available will depend on which exposure mode is selected via the mode dial and whether the built-in, or an external Speedlight is used.

To select a flash sync mode press the ⚡ and rotate the command dial; the mode is displayed in the control panel. To scroll through the flash sync modes available in the selected exposure mode continue to turn the command dial.

The plethora of flash sync modes available on the D50 may seem daunting, especially to the less experienced user. In all cases the ⚡ will appear in the control panel, and depending on the flash sync mode selected, additional icon(s) will also be displayed.

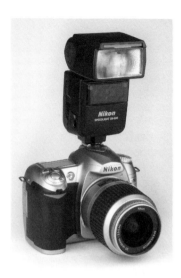

*The D50 with an*
*SB-600 Speedlight.*

## Built-In Speedlight with DVP Modes

In [AUTO icon] , [icon] , [icon] , and [icon] exposure modes you can select [AUTO icon] , [icon] , and [icon] .

In [icon] exposure mode you can select [icon] , [icon] , [icon] .

In [icon] , and [icon] the built-in Speedlight is disabled and [icon] is shown in the control panel.

## External Speedlight with DVP Modes

In [AUTO icon] , [icon] , [icon] , [icon] , [icon] , and [icon] exposure modes you can select either [icon] front curtain sync, or [icon] Red-eye reduction.

In [icon] exposure mode you can select either [insert SLOW icon] slow sync, or [icon] slow sync with red-eye reduction.

## Built-In and External Speedlights with P, S, A, and M Modes

In Program, and Aperture-priority exposure modes you can select [icon] , [icon] , [icon] , [icon] and [icon] .

In Shutter-priority and Manual exposure modes you can select 🗲 , ▭ , and ▭ .

▭ *Automatic Flash:* The built-in flash will lift automatically when the shutter release button is depress half-way but will only fire if the camera determines that additional lighting is required, for example, in low-light conditions or when the subject is backlit strongly.

🗲 *Front-Curtain Sync:* The flash fires as soon as the shutter has fully opened.

▭ *Red-Eye Reduction:* The D50 uses the AF-assist Lamp on the front right side of the camera body to light for approximately one second before the main exposure in an effort to reduce the size of the pupils in a subject's eyes.

▭ *Slow-Sync:* As soon as the shutter has fully opened, the flash fires at all shutter speeds between 30 seconds and 1/500th second regardless of the exposure mode used. Any image of a moving subject recorded by ambient light will appear to be in front of the flash-exposed subject.

▭ *Slow-Sync with Red-Eye:* Same as Slow-sync mode, except the Red-eye reduction lamp is switched on for approximately one second before the shutter opens in order to reduce pupil size.

**Rear-Curtain Sync:** In S and M exposure modes the flash fires just before the shutter closes at all shutter speeds between 30 seconds and 1/500th second. Any image of a moving subject recorded by ambient light will appear to be behind it. Thus, motion blurs will trail realistically behind the subject.

 **Slow Rear-Curtain Sync:** In P and A exposure modes, the flash fires at all shutter speeds between 30 seconds and 1/500th second just before the shutter closes. Any image of a moving subject recorded by ambient light will appear to be behind it.

 **Flash Off:** The flash is disabled and will not fire when the shutter release button is depressed fully to take a picture.

## Flash Sync Speed
The flash sync speed is the shutter speed or range of shutter speeds that are available when either the built-in Speedlight or an external Speedlight is used. The maximum flash sync speed of the D50 is 1/500s in all cases but the lowest flash sync speed depends on the selected exposure mode.

| Mode | Shutter speed |
|---|---|
| AUTO, 🏔, 🌸, P, A | $^1/_{500} - ^1/_{60}$ s |
| 🌷 | $^1/_{500} - ^1/_{125}$ s |
| 🌃 | $^1/_{500} - 1$ s |
| S, M | $^1/_{500} - 30$ s |

## Flash Exposure Compensation
Flash exposure compensation can be set on the D50 by pressing and holding both the **⚡** **☒** buttons while turning the command dial. Compensation can be set in increments of 1/3 or 1/2 EV (set via CS-11: EV Step) over a range of +1EV to −3EV (stops).

**Hint:** If you use the default i-TTL Balanced Fill-Flash mode, it will automatically set flash compensation based on scene brightness, contrast, focus distance, and a variety of other factors. The level of automatic adjustment applied by the D50 will often cancel any compensation factor you enter manually. Since there is no way of telling what the camera is doing, you will never have control of the flash exposure. To regain control, set the flash mode to Standard i-TTL by selecting M Exposure Mode, or Spot Metering in P, A, and S Exposure Modes.

*Note:* Flash compensation is not reset when the camera is turned off so remember to cancel flash compensation by re-setting the compensation factor to zero.

## FV Lock

If you want to take a flash-exposure when the main subject is not located in the center of the frame it is possible that the flash metering system may not provide an accurate reading. This can occur because the flash output is based entirely on the assessment of the monitor pre-flashes, and if the subject is positioned towards the edge of the frame area insufficient light from the pre-flashes may be reflected. The FV Lock allows you to trigger the pre-flashes without the main flash discharging. To activate this, you will need to, navigate to CS-14, and select the FV Lock option.

Confirm that the flash-ready signal is displayed in the viewfinder, and compose so that your subject is in the center of the frame, then press the shutter release half way to activate autofocus. Now press the AE-L/AF-L button to trigger the pre-flashes and allow the camera to calculate the flash exposure. It will lock this output value and EL will appear in the viewfinder display.

You can now recompose the shot, and take as many exposures as you like, because the flash output level will be locked (provided the camera meter remains active - if it switches off you will have to repeat the process). To release the FV lock option, press the AE-L/AF-L button again and confirm that EL is no longer displayed.

## Flash Range, Aperture, and Sensitivity (ISO)

This table shows the distance range covered by the D50's built-in Speedlight at different apertures and different sensitivity (ISO equivalent) values. For example, at an aperture of f/8 and an ISO of 400 the Speedlight is capable of illuminating a subject in the range of 2 to 8.75ft (0.6-2.7m).

| Aperture at ISO equivalent of | | | | Range | |
|---|---|---|---|---|---|
| 200 | 400 | 800 | 1600 | m | ft |
| 2 | 2.8 | 4 | 5.6 | 1.0–7.5 | 3'3"–24'7" |
| 2.8 | 4 | 5.6 | 8 | 0.7–5.4 | 2'4"–17'8" |
| 4 | 5.6 | 8 | 11 | 0.6–3.8 | 2'–12'6" |
| 5.6 | 8 | 11 | 16 | 0.6–2.7 | 2'–8'9" |
| 8 | 11 | 16 | 22 | 0.6–1.9 | 2'–6'3" |
| 11 | 16 | 22 | 32 | 0.6–1.4 | 2'–4'7" |
| 16 | 22 | 32 | – | 0.6–0.9 | 2'–2'11" |
| 22 | 32 | – | – | 0.6–0.7 | 2'–2'4" |

## Lens Compatibility

Generally, the built-in Speedlight of the D50 can be used with any CPU lens with a focal length of 18-300mm, and non-CPU (Ai-S, Ai, or Ai modified) lenses with a focal length of 18-200mm. However, due to the proximity of the built-in Speedlight to the central lens axis, there is a possibility that some lenses will obstruct the light emitted by the flash and cause uneven exposure. Likewise it is advisable to remove any lens hood to prevent the same problem occurring.

Nikon provides information for some specific lenses and state that when set to a particular focal length and used at or above the minimum shooting distances shown in the table opposite, the light from the built-in Speedlight may be obstructed.

| Lens | Zoom position | Minimum Range |
|---|---|---|
| AF-S DX ED 12–24mm f/4G | 20mm | 2.5m/8'2" |
| | 24mm | 1.0m/3'3" |
| AF-S ED 17–35mm f/2.8D | 20mm, 24mm | 2.5m/8'2" |
| | 28mm | 1.0m/3'3" |
| | 35mm | 0.6m/2' |
| AF-S DX IF ED 17–55mm f/2.8G | 20mm, 24mm | 2.5m/8'2" |
| | 28mm | 1.5m/4'11" |
| | 35mm | 0.7m/2'4" |
| | 45–55mm | 0.6m/2' |
| AF ED 18–35mm f/3.5–4.5D | 18mm, 21mm | 2.0m/6'7" |
| | 24mm | 0.7m/2'4" |
| | 28–35mm | 0.6m/2' |
| AF 20–35mm f/2.8D | 20mm | 1.5m/4'11" |
| | 24mm | 1.0m/3'3" |
| | 28–35mm | 0.6m/2' |
| AF-S VR ED 24–120mm f/3.5–5.6G | 24mm | 0.8m/2'7" |
| | 28–120mm | 0.6m/2' |
| AF-S ED 28–70mm f/2.8D | 28mm | 3.0m/9'10" |
| | 35mm | 1.0m/3'3" |
| | 50–70mm | 0.6m/2' |
| AF-S VR 200–400mm f/4G | 200mm | 4.0m/13'1" |
| | 250mm | 2.5m/8'2" |
| | 300–400mm | 0.6m/2' |
| AF-S 18–70mm f/3.5–4.5G | 18mm | 1.0m/3'3" |
| | 24–70mm | 0.6m/2' |

## External Speedlights

In addition to the built-in Speedlight, the D50 offers full i-TTL control with two external Speedlights: the SB-600 with a GN (at 35mm zoom-head position) 129/39 (ft/m, ISO 200) and the SB-800 with a GN (also at 35mm zoom-head position) 174/53 (ft/m, ISO 200).

Apart from being more powerful than the built-in unit, these two Speedlights are considerably more versatile since their flash heads can be tilted and swivelled for bounce flash. They also have an adjustable auto zoom-head (SB-800, 24-105mm) (SB-600, 24-85mm) that controls the angle-of-coverage of the flash beam, and a wide-angle diffuser for a focal length of 17mm (SB-800 only) and 14mm.

The i-TTL flash exposure control system only works with Nikon cameras and lenses that are compatible with the Creative Lighting System (CLS). The D50 does not support TTL flash exposure control with any other external Speedlights, other than the SB-600 and SB-800. When attached to a D50, either directly, or via the Nikon SC-28 or SC-29 TTL flash cords the SB-800 and SC-600 provide the following features:

| Speedlight / Flash mode/feature | SB-800 | SB-800 (Advanced Wireless Lighting) | SB-600 | SB-600 (Advanced Wireless Lighting) |
|---|---|---|---|---|
| i-TTL¹ | ✔² | ✔ | ✔² | ✔ |
| AA Auto aperture ¹ | ✔³ | ✔ | — | — |
| A Non-TTL auto | ✔³ | ✔⁴ | — | — |
| GN Range-priority manual | ✔⁵ | — | — | — |
| M Manual | ✔ | ✔ | ✔ | ✔ |
| RPT Repeating flash | ✔ | — | ✔ | — |
| REAR Rear-curtain sync | ✔ | ✔ | ✔ | ✔ |
| 👁 Red-eye reduction | ✔ | — | ✔ | — |
| Flash Color Information Communication | ✔ | — | ✔³ | — |
| FV lock¹ | ✔ | ✔ | ✔ | ✔ |
| AF-assist for multi-area AF ⁶ | ✔ | — | ✔ | — |
| Auto zoom ¹ | ✔ | — | ✔ | — |
| ISO Auto (Custom Setting 10) ¹ | ✔ | — | ✔ | — |

¹ Available only with CPU lenses (IX Nikkor lenses excluded).
² Standard i-TTL Flash for Digital SLR is used when spot metering is selected. Otherwise, i-TTL Balanced Fill-Flash for Digital SLR is used.
³ Use Speedlight controls to select flash mode.
⁴ Available only with non-CPU lenses.
⁵ Adjusted automatically according to camera aperture setting when CPU lens is used. When non-CPU lens is used, must be adjusted manually to match aperture selected with lens aperture ring.
⁶ Available only with CPU AF lenses only (IX Nikkor lenses excluded).

Other external Nikon Speedlights can be attached and used with the D50. However, the camera will only support non-TTL standard automatic flash mode, where the built-in sensor of the relevant Speedlight controls flash output, or manual flash mode. If you set any of these Speedlights to TTL the shutter release button of the D50 will be disabled and the flash will not be triggered.

*The shadow from the flash is, again, used for its dramatic effect. In this case, the shadow from direct flash accents the shape of the leaf and makes it pop.* ⇨

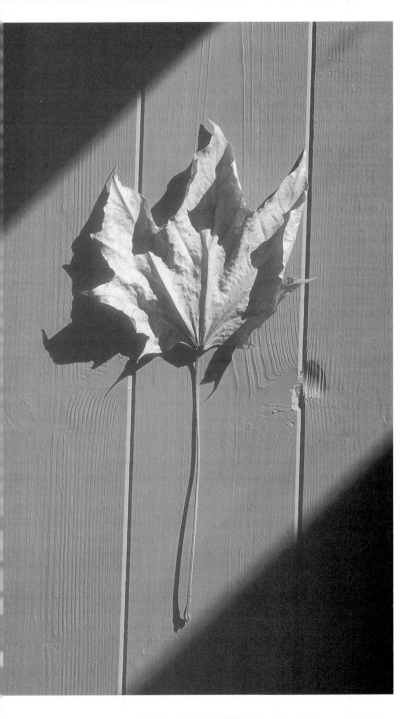

## Maximum Aperture With External Speedlights

If you attach an external Speedlight to the D50 and use the camera in P, ▣ᴬᵁᵀᴼ , 🏃 , 🌼 , 🌷 , 🏔 , and 🏃 modes the maximum lens aperture (smallest f/ number) is limited according to the sensitivity (ISO). Unless the value of the maximum lens aperture is less (larger f/ number) than the value shown in the table below in which case the maximum shooting aperture is that of the lens.

| Mode | Maximum aperture at ISO equivalent of | | | |
| --- | --- | --- | --- | --- |
| | 200 | 400 | 800 | 1600 |
| P, ▣ᴬᵁᵀᴼ, 🏃, 🏔, 🌷, 🏃, 📷 | 4 | 4.8 | 5.6 | 6.7 |
| 🌼 | 8 | 9.5 | 11 | 13 |

*Note:* It is important to remember this point, as lens aperture has a profound affect on the appearance of a picture.

**Hint:** Unlike earlier Nikon Speedlights that cancelled monitor pre-flashes if the flash head was tilted or swivelled for bounce flash photography, the SB-800 and SB-600 emit pre-flashes regardless of the flash head orientation to help improve the accuracy of flash exposure.

## Additional Flash Modes

*(AA) Auto Aperture (SB-800 Only):* In this mode the SB-800 reads the sensitivity (ISO) setting and lens aperture from the D50 automatically, and receives the fire flash signal from the camera as well. It can be used in A and M exposure modes. When the flash is fired during the exposure, a sensor on the front panel of the Speedlight monitors the flash exposure and as soon as this sensor detects that the flash output has been sufficient, the flash pulse is quenched. If, between exposures, you decide to alter the focal length or change the lens aperture, the Speedlight will adjust its output accordingly to maintain a correct flash exposure. The problem with this option is that it is not TTL, so the sensor does not necessarily see the same scene as the lens, which can lead to inaccurate exposure.

**Hint:** The focal lengths indicated on Speedlight zoom heads assume the unit is attached to a film camera, not a digital SLR like the D50 with its reduced angle-of-view due to its smaller (than full 35mm film frame) sensor. Therefore, if you don't compensate, the flash will illuminate a greater area than is required when used on the D50. This has the effect of reducing the flash shooting distance, squandering flash power, and draining the battery unnecessarily. Use the following table to maximize the performance of an external Speedlight:

| Focal length of lens (mm) | Zoom head position (mm) |
|---|---|
| 14 | 20 |
| 18 | 24 |
| 20 | 28 |
| 24 | 35 |
| 28 | 50 |
| 35 | 50 |
| 50 | 70 |
| 70 | 85 |
| 85 | 105 [1] |

*[1] - Available on SB-800 only.*

*(A) Automatic Non-TTL (SB-800 only):* This mode can be used in A and M camera exposure modes. Similar to the AA mode, a sensor on the front of the SB-800 monitors flash levels and shuts off the flash when the Speedlight calculates that sufficient light has been emitted. However, the lens aperture and sensitivity (ISO) values must be set manually on the Speedlight to ensure the subject is within the flash shooting range. As with the AA mode, the sensor does not necessarily see the same scene as the lens, which can lead to inaccurate exposure.

*The extra two contacts on the foot of the SB-600 Speedlight connect the AF-assist Lamp of the SC-29 to the Speedlight's power source.*

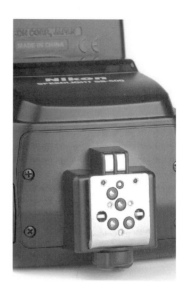

## Taking Flash Off Camera

Mounting a flash on the hot shoe immediately above the lens places it in an unfavourable position because it produces flat, frontal lighting with no modelling. Generally, far better results can be achieved by taking the flash off the camera. To maintain full i-TTL control, Nikon produces the SC-28 TTL remote cord and the SC-29 TTL connecting cord with a built-in AF-assist Lamp, both 4.9 feet (1.5m) long.

Nikon state that if you use an SB-800 or SB-600 off camera via the SC-28 or SC-29 flash exposure in the i-TTL mode may not be accurate. This is because the i-TTL system assumes the flash is mounted on the camera and is therefore at the same distance from the subject, which is important as the focus distance is taken in to consideration during the flash exposure calculations. If you take the flash off the camera via a TTL cord then obviously the distance between the flash and the subject may differ from the distance between the camera and the subject. In this situation there is a risk the flash exposure may be incorrect, so always ensure that the flash and camera are at approximate the same distance from the subject when using off camera flash.

To connect the D50 to non-dedicated flash units such as AC powered studio lights via a standard flash synchronisation cord that connects to a PC socket, you will need to fit the Nikon AS-15 PC Sync adapter to the accessory shoe connector of the D50.

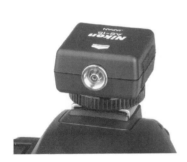

*The AS-15 PC Sync adapter attaches to the hot shoe of the camera. It accepts standard PC plugs and allows a non-dedicated flash to sync properly with the camera through a connection in the hot shoe.*

## Wireless TTL Flash Control

The built-in Speedlight flash unit of the D50 does not support the wireless TTL flash control capabilities of Nikon's Creative Lighting System. However it is possible to use the D50 for wireless flash control of multiple Speedlights (SB-800 or SB-600 only) if you attach an SB-800 and use it in its Commander mode.

The full wireless CLS flash system using an external SB-800 Speedlight as the master unit in its Commander mode can support the control of up to three sub-groups of

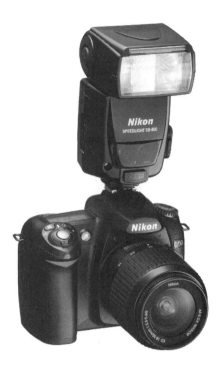

*An SB-800 Speedlight in Commander mode mounted on the Nikon D50 will act as a "master unit" to fire other SB-800s or SB-600s in a wireless flash set up.*

remote Speedlights, each using a different flash exposure control mode if desired. You can also choose between four different communication channels to avoid interference problems from other photographers using Nikon's CLS wireless i-TTL flash control system.

*Note:* The SB-600 can only be used as a remote (slave) flash unit.

The master Speedlight (Commander mode) communicates with the remote Speedlight(s) by transmitting a series of light pulses (think of it as a sort of Morse code) using light that is in the near infrared wavelength range. As such these very rapid pulses are imperceptible.

In most instances you will want to select TTL Mode with either the SB-800 or SB-600 since this provides the most sophisticated level of flash exposure control, although you can remotely control the flash units in either (AA) Auto Aperture (SB-800 only) or (M) Manual flash (SB-800 or SB-600).

Nikon recommends that you set each remote Speedlight unit (SB-600 and SB-800 only) so that its wireless control sensor, located on the lower right side of the main Speedlight body, has a line-of-sight to the D50's built-in Speedlight. Furthermore, they suggest that the remote Speedlight(s) should be no more than 33 feet (10m) when it is placed directly in front of the camera; or between no more than 16 feet (5m) to 23ft (7) from the camera when the remote Speedlight(s) up to a maximum angle of 30° away from the camera-to-subject axis.

In practice I have found these recommendations to be somewhat conservative. Provided you are working with the remote flash at a relatively short range (no more than about 16 feet (5m), particularly where the level of ambient light is rather low, such as indoors), and there are surfaces in proximity to the remote flash unit from which the control signals of the Commander flash unit can be reflected, it is possible to position the remote Speedlight or Speedlights out of sight of the camera. Though you will need to experiment with your proposed lighting set-up, it is possible to light a background or backlight a subject without a direct line-of-sight between the D50 and its SB-800 Commander flash and the remote Speedlight(s).

Once you have made the necessary settings, you can shoot away and move camera position (provided the trigger signal from the built-in Speedlight can be received by the sensor(s) on the remote Speedlight(s)), change focal length and/or lens aperture, and the system will maintain full i-TTL control of the flash exposure.

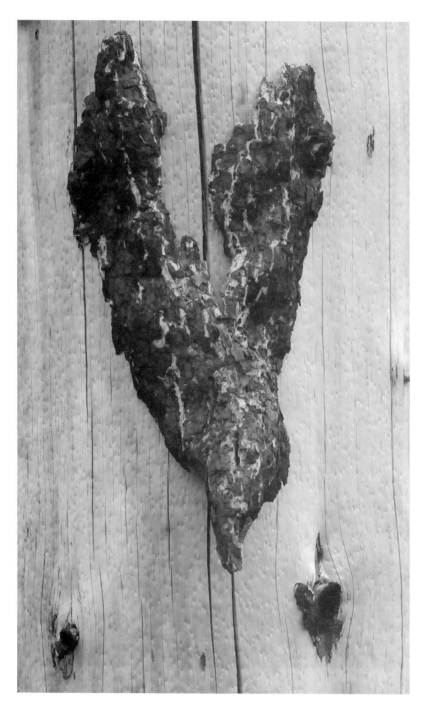

# Nikon Lenses
# and Accessories

The Nikon F mount created for Nikkor lenses (Nikon's trademark for its lenses) is legendary. Since the introduction of the original Nikon F in 1959 the F mount has been retained on all Nikon 35mm film and digital SLR cameras. Since it is virtually unchanged, a great many of the lenses produced by Nikon over the past four decades can be mounted on the D50.

## DX-Format Sensor

All Nikon digital SLR cameras, to date, have the same size sensor. Called the DX-format, the size is .61 x .93 inches (15.6 x 23.7 mm), which is smaller than a 35mm film frame. Because of this, the field-of-view seen by the D50 is reduced by about 1.5x compared with that seen by 35mm film camera.

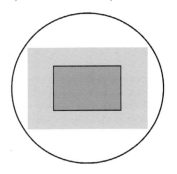

*The outside pale gray rectangle is the image area for a 35mm film frame (24 x 36 mm), and the inner dark gray rectangle represents the area covered by the DX-format (15.6 x 23.7 mm) sensor used in the D50. (Diagram not shown to scale).*

☜ *Zooms make it possible to shoot many different subjects without changing lenses. Wide-angle to telephoto zooms are especially versatile and can handle everything from landscapes to small details and portraits.*

Marketing people like to extol positives rather than negatives! Hence, advertising claims that it is like getting a free 1.5x teleconverter or a more powerful lens have instilled the notion (even among those who should know better) that the focal length of a 35mm format lens in some way magically increases by 1.5x when attached to a DX-format Nikon digital SLR. This is not correct. A 300mm lens on a Nikon 35mm film camera is still a 300mm lens on the D50—no ifs or buts! Furthermore, a teleconverter generally reduces image sharpness and contrast, but since no extra glass is required to achieve the D50's image, these issues are irrelevant.

It is the field-of-view rather than the focal length that actually changes, and in fact, it is decreased (there's that negative aspect!). Consequently, a 35mm lens on the D50 see's a field-of-view equivalent to a focal length 1.5x greater. If you were to shoot two pictures of exactly the same subject with the same lens using a D50 and a film SLR, then cropped the film image to the same area as the sensor in the D50, you would end up with identical pictures.

The following table gives the approximate focal length equivalent for a 35mm format lens when mounted on the D50:

| Picture angle | Approximate focal length (mm) in 35mm format (modified for picture angle) | | | | | | | |
|---|---|---|---|---|---|---|---|---|
| 35mm film camera | 17 | 20 | 24 | 28 | 35 | 50 | 60 | 85 |
| D50 | 25.5 | 30 | 36 | 42 | 52.5 | 75 | 90 | 127.5 |
| 35mm film camera | 105 | 135 | 180 | 200 | 300 | 400 | 500 | 600 |
| D50 | 157.5 | 202.5 | 270 | 300 | 450 | 600 | 750 | 900 |

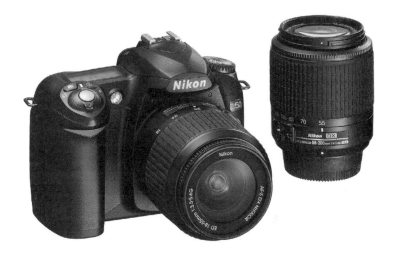

*Nikon's 18-55mm DX Zoom lens is called a "kit" lens because it is often offered as an outfit with the D50 body. If you buy this kit you will get a lot of versatility at an economical price.*

## Choosing a Lens

There is a beneficial side effect of this reduced angle-of-view. Since the sensor of the D50 is only using the central portion of the total image projected by a lens designed for 35mm film cameras, the effects of optical aberrations and defects are kept to a minimum since these are generally more prevalent toward the edge of the image circle. All of the following tend to be significantly reduced if not eliminated altogether:

- Light fall-off toward the edge and corners of the image area
- Chromatic aberration
- Linear distortion—both barrel and pin-cushion
- Flat field focus
- Vignetting with filters

Wide-angle lenses offer a large field-of-view. Typically they are associated with landscape photography where they can be used to capture a sweeping vista, but wide-angles are great for many subjects. Their close-focusing ability, extended depth of field, and broad angle-of-view can be combined to create dynamic compositions with a dominant subject in the foreground set against an expansive backdrop.

Telephoto lenses provide a reduced angle-of-view that magnifies a subject, making them good for sport, action, and wildlife photography when it is usually difficult to get close to the subject. The optical effects of a telephoto can be used in many other areas of photography, such a portrait and landscape as they can help isolate a subject from its background due to their limited depth of field, particularly at large apertures.

Zoom lenses allow you to adjust the focal length, the range of which can be exclusively wide-angle, telephoto, or both. Zoom lenses are extremely versatile because you have several focal lengths available in one lens, which reduces the number of lenses you need to carry, letting you spend less time changing lenses. However, convenience comes at a price; many zoom lenses have smaller maximum apertures, often two-stops less compared with fixed-focal length lenses. This can be an issue when shooting in low light. Zoom lenses with large maximum apertures (small f/numbers) tend to be expensive due to the complexity of their optical engineering. For general photography with the D50, a couple of D or G-type zoom lenses that offer focal lengths between 18mm and 200mm will cover most shooting situations, and provide total compatibility with all the features and functions of the camera.

Nikon makes a huge range of lenses. The following table provides details of the compatibility of the various types available:

| Lens / accessory | Focus | | | Mode | | Metering | | |
|---|---|---|---|---|---|---|---|---|
| **Camera setting** → | **AF** | **M** (with electronic range finder) | **M** | **DVP, P, S, A** | **M** | **3D** | **Color** | ⊙ / • |
| *CPU lenses[1]* | | | | | | | | |
| Type G or D AF Nikkor[2] / AF-S, AF-I Nikkor | ● | ● | ● | ● | ● | ● | — | ●[3] |
| PC-Micro Nikkor 85mm f/2.8D[4] | — | ●[5] | ● | — | ● | ● | — | ●[3] |
| AF-S/AF-I Teleconverter[6] | ●[7] | ●[7] | ● | ● | ● | ● | — | ●[3] |
| Other AF Nikkor (except lenses for F3AF) | ●[8] | ●[8] | ● | ● | ● | — | ● | ●[3] |
| AI-P Nikkor | — | ●[9] | ● | ● | ● | — | ● | ●[3] |
| *Non-CPU lenses[10]* | | | | | | | | |
| AI-, AI-S, or Series E Nikkor / AI modified Nikkor | — | ●[9] | ● | — | ●[11] | — | — | — |
| Medical Nikkor 120mm f/4 | — | ● | ● | — | ●[12] | — | — | — |
| Reflex Nikkor | — | — | ● | — | ●[11] | — | — | — |
| PC-Nikkor | — | ●[5] | ● | — | ●[11] | — | — | — |
| AI-type Teleconverter | — | ●[7] | ● | — | ●[11] | — | — | — |
| PB-6 Bellows Focusing Attachment[13] | — | ●[7] | ● | — | ●[11] | — | — | — |
| Auto extension rings (PK-series 11-A, 12, or 13; PN-11) | — | ●[7] | ● | — | ●[11] | — | — | — |

*1 IX Nikkor lenses can not be used.*

*2 Vibration Reduction (VR) supported with VR lens.*

*3 Spot metering meters selected focus area.*

*4 The camera's exposure metering and flash control systems do not work properly when shifting and/or tilting the lens, or when an aperture other than the maximum aperture is used.*

*5 Electronic range finder can not be used with shifting or tilting.*

*6 Compatible with AF-I Nikkor lenses and with all AF-S lenses except DX 12-24mm f/4G, ED 17-35mm f/2.8D, DX 17-55mm f/2.8G, DX ED 18-70mm f3.5-4.5G, ED 24-85mm f/3.5-4.5G, VR ED 24-120mm f/3.5-5.6G and ED 28-70mm f/2.8D.*

*7 With maximum effective aperture of f/5.6 or faster*

*8 If AF 80-200mm f/2.8, AF 35-70mm f/2.8, new-model AF 28-85mm f/3.5-4.5, or AF 28-85mm f/3.5-4.5, is zoomed in while focusing at minimum range, image on matte screen in viewfinder may not in focus when in-focus indicator is displayed. Focus manually using image in viewfinder as guide.*

*9 With maximum aperture of f/5.6 or faster.*

*10 Some lenses can not be used.*

*11 Can be used in mode M, but camera exposure meter can not be used.*

*12 Can be used in mode M at shutter speeds slower than 1/125s, but camera exposure meter can not be used.*

*13 Attach in vertical orientation (can be used in horizontal orientation once attached).*

*• Medical Nikkor 200mm f/5.6 requires AS-15 for flash control.*

## Incompatible Accessories and Non-CPU Lenses

The following accessories and non-CPU lenses can NOT be used with the D50:

- TC-16A AF Teleconverter
- Non-AI lenses
- Lenses that require the AU-1 focusing unit (400mm f/4.5, 600mm f/5.6, 800mm f/8, 1200mm f/11)
- Fisheye (6mm f/5.6, 8mm f/8, OP 10mm f/5.6)
- 21mm f/4 (old type)
- K2 rings
- ED 180-600mm f/8 (serial numbers 174041-174180)
- ED 360-1200mm f/il (serial numbers 174031-174127)
- 200-600mm f/9.5 (serial numbers 280001-300490)
- Lenses for the F3AF (80mm f/2.8, 200mm f/3.5, TC-16 Teleconverter)
- PC 28mm f/4 (serial number 180900 or earlier)
- PC 35mm f/2.8 (serial numbers 851001- 906200)
- PC 35mm f/3.5 (old type)
- 1000mm f/6.3 Reflex (old type)
- 1000mm f/11 Reflex (serial numbers 142361-143000)
- 2000mm f/11 Reflex (serial numbers 200111-200310)

## Compatible Non-CPU Lenses

Non-CPU lenses not in the list above can only be used in M (Manual) Mode. Aperture must be adjusted manually using the lens aperture ring. The camera exposure meter, depth-of-field-preview, and i-TTL flash control cannot be used.

*Note:* The shutter release button is disabled if a mode other than M is selected when using a non-CPU lens.

# Features of Nikkor Lenses

The designation of Nikkor lenses, particularly modern auto-focus types, is peppered with initials. Here is an explanation as to what some of these stand for:

- **D-type**—These lenses have a conventional aperture ring and an electronic chip that communicates information about lens aperture and focus distance between the lens and the camera body.

- **G-type**—Noteable due to the fact that these lenses have no aperture ring and are only compatible with Nikon cameras that allow the aperture value to be set from the camera body. They do contain an electronic chip that communicates information about lens aperture and focus distance between the lens and the camera body, similar to the D-type lenses.

- **DX**—Lenses in the DX-Nikkor range have been especially designed for use on Nikon D-SLR cameras. They project a smaller image circle compared with a 35mm format lens, but the light exiting their rear element is more collimated to improve the efficiency of the photo sites on the camera's sensor.

- **AF-S**—Not to be confused with Single-servo autofocus, AF-S denotes the lens has a silent-wave focusing motor that uses alternating magnetic fields to move the lens elements to adjust focus. This system offers the fastest auto-focusing of all AF Nikkor lenses.

- **VR**—Vibration Reduction lenses have an electro-optical system that helps reduce the effect of camera shake to help improve image sharpness.

- **ED**—Developed by Nikon Extra-low Dispersion glass reduces the effect of chromatic aberration by bring various wavelengths of light to a common point of focus.

- **IF**—To speed up focusing, particularly with long focal length lenses, Nikon developed their internal focusing (IF) system. This moves a group of elements within the lens so that it does not change in length during focusing, and prevents the front filter mount from rotating, which facilitates use of filters such as a polarizer.

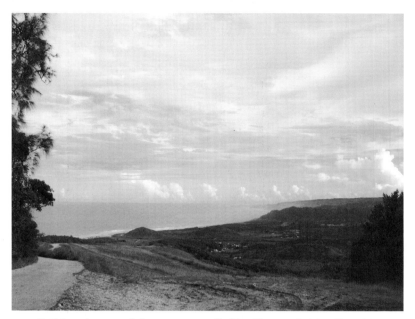

*Nothing gives you "picture postcard" skies like a polarizing filter. It is probably the most useful filter you can buy for digital photography. ©Mimi Netzel*

## Filters

The D50's white balance control obviates the need to carry a range of color correction and color compensating filters that you would normally need when shooting on film. However, filters are an integral part of any digital photographer's equipment, because there are a few filter effects that you simply cannot replicate using a computer; the good news is you do not need a great many! I would recommend that you consider the following three types.

### Polarizing Filter
Probably the most useful and well-known filter is a polarizer. Often associated with its ability to deepen the color of a blue sky, a polarizer has many other uses. The polarizer's unique effect is one that makes it an essential filter for film

or digital. Since it can remove reflections from non-metallic surfaces, including water, it is a favorite with landscape photographers. Even on a dull overcast day, a polarizer can help reduce the glare from foliage, thereby intensifying color.

**Hint:** The D50's autofocus and metering systems will not function properly with a linear-type polarizing filter; you must use a circular-type polarizer.

## Neutral Density Filters
The D50's relatively high base sensitivity of ISO 200 often means that in bright light you cannot set a lens aperture or shutter speed to achieve the required results. Continuous tone neutral density filters help to reduce the overall exposure so you can use longer shutter speeds and/or wider apertures under these conditions.

## Graduated Neutral Density Filters
Coping with excessive contrast is one of the most difficult aspects of digital photography. For example, the sky is often much brighter than the land, even at each end of the day, which can make shooting landscapes tricky. Graduated neutral density filters, clear on one side and becoming progressively denser toward the other, are the ideal solution. They come in a variety of strengths and gradients. If you use a slot-in type of filter system, it is easy to align these graduated filters so their dense area darkens the sky, leaving the clear portion over the foreground area.

*Note:* Nikon does not produce graduated neutral density filters.

**Hint:** Nikon states that the 3D Color Matrix and color Matrix metering of the D50 is not recommended when using any filter with a filter factor over 1x. The filter factor is the amount of exposure compensation required to adjust for the reduction in light transmission caused by the filter. For example, a filter factor of 2x is equivalent to one-stop; a factor of 8x is equivalent to three-stops. This applies to dense filters such as polarizing and neutral density filters. The best solution is to switch to Center-weighted or Spot metering.

## General Accessories

- **2370 Eyepiece adapter**—This allows viewfinder accessories with a round attachment thread to be mounted on the D50's square viewfinder eyepiece.

- **AS-15**—An adapter that mounts into the camera's hot shoe, providing a connection to standard PC sync lead.

- **BF-1A**—This is a body cap that will help prevent dust from entering the camera.

*Note:* The earlier BF-1 type cap should not be used because it may damage the lens mount.

- **BM-5**—LCD Monitor screen cover for the D50.

- **DG-2**—Viewfinder eyepiece magnifier that provides an approximate 2x magnification of the central area of the viewfinder field.

*Note:* Requires the Eyepiece adapter to be fitted.

- **DK-5**—Viewfinder eyepiece cover, which prevents light from entering the viewfinder and affecting exposure measurement.

- **DK-3**—Circular rubber eyecup for the Nikon FM3A that can be attached via the square-to-circular viewfinder accessory Eyepiece adapter. It requires a viewfinder eyepiece filter for the FM3A camera to hold it in place. The circular eyecup provides a better light seal when held to the photographer's eye orbit than the D50's standard square eyecup.

- **DK-20**—Rectangular viewfinder eyecup (supplied with the D50) is also compatible with D70s/D70 camera.

*A close-up lens set will allow you to get in close without spending a lot of money and can greatly expand your photography. Basically magnifying lenses in threaded filter mounts, they attach easily to the front of a lens.*

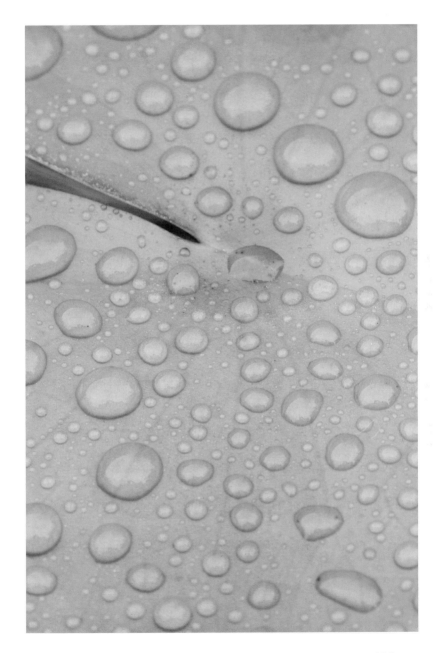

195

- **DR-6**—Right angle viewer which attaches directly to the square frame of the D50's viewfinder eyepiece. It is useful when the camera is at a low shooting position.

- **EH-5**—Multi-voltage AC adapter for powering the D50.

- **EN-EL3**—7.4 v/1400 mAh rechargeable Lithium ion battery (supplied with the D50).

- **EN-EL3a**—7.4 v/1500 mAh rechargeable Lithium ion battery. This battery offers approximately 25% more shooting capacity than the EN-EL3.

- **MH-18**—Multi-voltage AC charger for a single EN-EL3 or EN-EL3a battery.

- **MH-18a**—Compact version of the MH-18 multi-voltage AC charger for a single EN-EL3 or EN-EL3a battery.

- **MH-19**—Multiple battery charger that can charge two EN-EL3/3a batteries and supports either a multi-voltage AC supply or 12V DC motor vehicle supply.

- **ML-L1 Remote**—An infra red remote release that can be substituted for the ML-L3.

- **ML-L3 Remote**—An infrared remote release for the D50. It requires a CR2025 battery.

- **Nikon Capture 4**—Offers full support for Nikon NEF files. The D50 requires version 4.3 or higher. The Nikon Editor application can be used to transfer images to a computer, view, edit, and print them. The Nikon Camera Control application permits remote control of a camera via a USB cable connection.

- **Nikon View 6**—Provides transfer and browsing features for importing and organizing your pictures in a computer. It also provides limited editing controls for NEF RAW files, which is something the current version of Picture Project (1.5.2) lacks.

- **Teleconverters TC-14E II, TC-17E II, and TC-20E II**—
These small optical devices fit between the lens and camera body to magnify the image. They are available in three different strengths (1.4x, 1.7x, and 2.0x). They reduce the maximum effective aperture of the lens, but retain the minimum focus distance.

## Memory Card Compatibility

Nikon has tested and approved the use of the following SD (Secure Digital) cards with the D50:

SanDisk 64MB, 128MB, 256MB, 512 MB and 1GB

SanDisk Ultra II 512 MB*

Panasonic 64MB, 128MB, 256MB, 512 MB and 1GB

Panasonic Super High Speed 256MB*, 512 MB* and 1GB*

Panasonic Pro High Speed 512 MB* and 1GB*

Toshiba (blue) 64MB, 128MB, 256MB and 512MB

Toshiba (white) 128MB*, 256MB* and 512MB*

*These cards support a data transfer rate of 10MB/s or more.*

Other brands and capacities of SD cards will probably work, but Nikon does not guarantee they will operate properly. So, if you use a memory card not listed above please check with the manufacturer for compatibility with the D50. Since card compatibility can be an issue Nikon recommend keeping an approved memory card available in case you need to do some troubleshooting.

*Note:* Multi Media cards (MMC) are not recommended and should not be used.

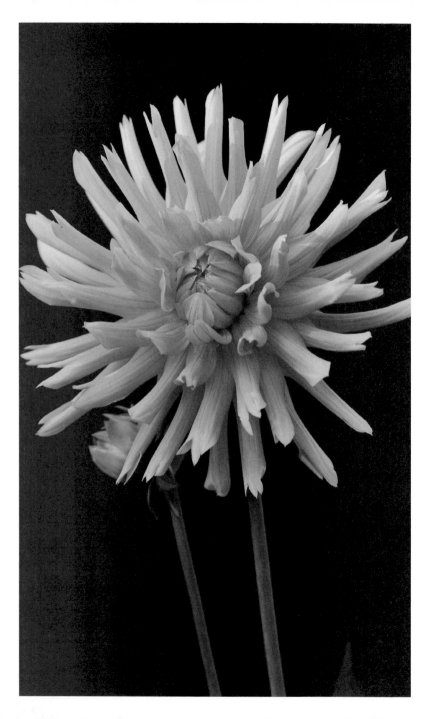

# Working with Pictures

## Image Information

You may be surprised to learn that, in addition to image data, the picture files generated by the D50 contain a wealth of other information that includes the shooting parameters and instructions about printing pictures.

### Exchangeable Image File Format (EXIF)
The D50 uses the EXIF standard for embedding information within the image file (sometimes this information is referred to as metadata, which is a more generic term). The firmware of the D50 supports EXIF version 2.21 (since firmware and software can be updated at any time, check with Nikon to insure you have the latest versions available). The EXIF file holds the following information on each image file:

- Nikon (the name of the camera manufacturer).

- D50 (the model number).

- Camera firmware version number.

- Exposure information, including shutter speed, aperture, exposure mode, ISO, exposure value, date/time, exposure compensation, flash mode, and focal length.

- Thumbnail of the main image.

&#9685; *Sometimes called "metadata" the information embedded in an image file provides a record of the camera settings used to make the photo such as exposure, shutter speed, aperture, ISO, and more.*

You can examine EXIF data by either viewing the image information pages displayed on the LCD monitor screen of the camera, or accessing it via Nikon software (in Nikon Capture and Nikon View click on the Shooting Data tab, and in Nikon PictureProject open the View menu and select Display > List. Checking the shooting data is a great teaching aid because you can see exactly what the camera settings were for each shot. By comparing pictures and the shooting data, you can quickly learn about the technical aspects of exposure, focusing, metering and flash exposure control.

## International Press Telecommunications Council (IPTC)

Many image processing applications, including Nikon PictureProject, Nikon View and Nikon Capture (see page XXX), allow further information to be tagged to the image file. The International Press Telecommunications Council (IPTC) has developed a standard known as Digital Newsphoto Parameter Record (DNPR), which can carry additional image information including origin, authorship, copyright, captions, and key words for searching purposes. The camera itself does not write any DNPR metadata to its image files; that is done by other applications.

*Note:* Many people and applications, including Nikon software, refer erroneously to DNPR as the "IPTC data" but as long as you understand its worth using the correct name is less important.

Any application that is DNPR compliant will show this information and allow you to edit it. However, if you are considering submitting pictures for publication, you should make use of DNPR metadata, as most publishing organizations require it to be present before accepting a submission.

*You can download pictures directly from the D50 to your computer using Nikon PictureProject software and the UC-E4 USB cable, which come with the camera. Make sure you have a fully charged battery so that you don't unintentionally damage the SD card or your images by a loss of power during the transfer process.*

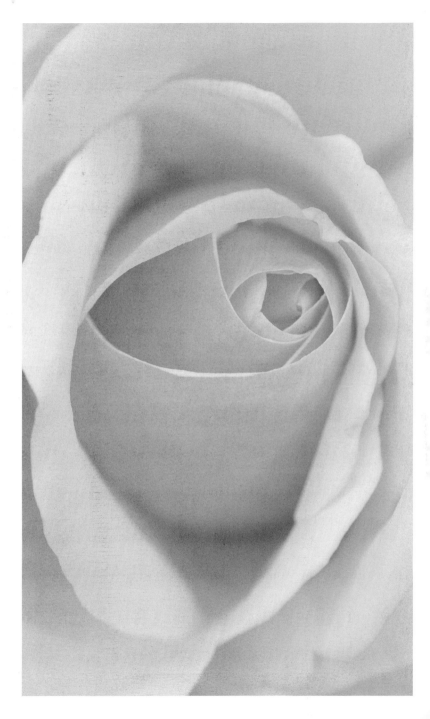

## Camera Connections

### Connecting to a TV or Video Monitor

The D50 can be connected to a television set or VCR for playback or recording of images by using the EG-D100 video cable. First, you need to select the appropriate video standard. NTSC is the video standard used in the USA, Canada, and Japan. PAL is used in most European countries.

Press the [MENU] button and navigate to the Set-up Menu and highlight Video Mode. Press ⓘ and select either NTSC or PAL. Now switch the camera off.

*The external ports of the D50 are beneath the rubber cover on the left side of the camera body, and include the DC-in, Video-out, and USB connector.*

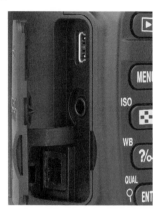

To connect the camera, make sure its power is switched OFF. Open the large rubber cover on the left end of the camera body to reveal the ports for DC-in ( bottom) and Video out (center), then connect the narrow jack-pin of the EG-D100 to the camera and the other end to the TV/VCR. Tune the TV to the video channel, and turn on the camera. The image that would normally be displayed on the LCD Monitor will be shown on the television screen or recorded to videotape.

*Note:* The LCD Monitor will remain blank but all other camera operations will function normally. So, you can take pictures with the camera connected to a TV set or video monitor and carry out review/playback functions as you would with the LCD Monitor.

**Connecting to a Computer**

The D50 can be connected directly to a computer via the supplied USB cable (UC-E4). This supports the High-Speed USB (2.0) interface with a maximum transfer rate of 480 Mbps. You can download images from the camera using the supplied Nikon PictureProject software, Nikon View available separately, or alternatively by setting camera controls and operating the camera from a computer using the Camera Control functions of the optional Nikon Capture 4.3 software.

**Hint:** If you use the D50 connected to a computer for any function, be sure that the EN-EL3/3a battery is fully charged. If you expect to use the camera in this way for protracted periods it is probably better to use the EH-5 AC adapter to prevent loss or corruption of data during transfer by loss of power.

Before connecting the D50 to a computer, either one of the Nikon applications mentioned above, or an appropriate third party application suitable for data transfer must be installed, and the camera should be configured for one of the following two options: M – Mass Storage or P – PTP. To do this open the Setup Menu and navigate to the USB option. Press ⌣ to display the two options; M (Mass storage) and P (PTP). Highlight the appropriate option (see descriptions below) and press ⌣ to set it.

*Mass Storage:* In this configuration the D50 acts like a card reader and the computer sees the memory card in the camera as an external disk drive. This is the default setting and it only allows the computer to read the data on the memory card. Use this option if your computer is running Windows (98SE, Me, or 2000 Pro).

*Note:* If Mass Storage is selected as the USB option PC will be displayed in the control panel and viewfinder. No icon appears if PTP is selected.

*Note:* If you only require data to be moved from your camera to a computer you can use the Mass Storage option with Windows XP (Home and Professional) or Macintosh OS X (10.4.1 or later).

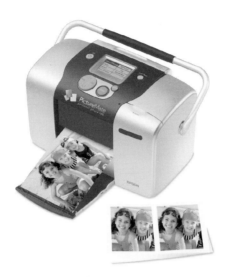

*Digital "instant" photography is just a push of the button away with this fun, take-along direct printer from Epson. Take one to your next party or family gathering and enjoy one of the most fun parts of owning a digital camera—sharing pictures. ©Epson America, Inc.*

***Picture Transfer Protocol (PTP):*** In this configuration the D50 acts like another device on a computer network and the computer can communicate and control camera operations. Use this option if you want to use the camera control features in Nikon Capture 4.3 using Windows XP (Home and Professional) or Macintosh OS X (10.4.1 or later).

To connect the camera to the computer using the UC-E4 lead, first make sure the camera is switched OFF. Open the rubber cover on the left end of the camera and plug in the appropriate end of the UC-E4 (the plugs on each end are unique so you can only connect the lead one-way). Turn the camera ON and the computer should recognize the camera and launch the installed Nikon software.

The D50 will continue to operate normally when tethered to a computer so you can shoot and download images directly, as well as control the camera using Nikon Capture 4.3 software.

## Disconnecting the Camera

It is essential that a D50 camera that is connected to a computer be disconnected in the correct manner.

If you have PTP selected as the USB option the camera can be switched off and the USB cord disconnected once data transfer is complete. However, if the Mass Storage USB option is used the procedure for disconnection will vary according to the computer operating system in use (see table below)

| Operating System | Method |
|---|---|
| **Windows XP Home /Professional** | Click the "Safely Remove Hardware" icon in the taskbar and select Safely remove USB Mass Storage Device from the menu |
| **Windows 2000 Professional** | Click the "Unplug or Eject Hardware" icon in the taskbar and select Stop USB Mass Storage Device from the menu |
| **Windows Millennium Edition** | Click the "Unplug or Eject Hardware: icon in the taskbar and select Stop USB Disk from the menu |
| **Window 98 Second Edition** | Go to My Computer, right click on the removable disk that corresponds to the camera and select Eject from the menu |
| **Macintosh OS X** | Drag the volume "Nikon D50" to the Trash can icon in the Dock |

## Card Readers

Card readers are an inexpensive and simple way to download images from memory card. They are readily available at stores that sell digital cameras and computers. Most photographers prefer this method of downloading for the following reasons:

• If you use the linked camera method, you will drain battery power with a risk that data could be lost or corrupted if the power fails.

- Using a card reader allows you to run software to recover lost or corrupted image files as well as diagnose problems with the memory card.

- You can leave a card reader permanently attached to your computer, which further reduces the risk of losing or corrupting files as a result of a poor connection due to the wear and tear caused by constantly connecting the camera.

## Printing Pictures

Pictures recorded with your D50 can be printed by a variety of methods.

- Connecting the camera directly to a printer and printing pictures from the camera

- Taking the SD memory card out of the camera and inserting it directly in to a compatible printer (if the printer support DPOF you can select pictures for printing using the Print Set option in the Playback menu).

- Taking the SD memory card to a commercial digital printing facility (if the printer support DPOF you can select pictures for printing using the Print Set option in the Playback menu).

- Transferring the pictures from the memory card to a computer and printing them via a compatible printer, from Nikon Picture Project, Nikon View, Nikon Capture, or other third party application.

## Direct Printing

The D50 allows you to select a set of images that can be printed directly by either connecting the camera to a compatible printer or inserting the memory card into a compatible printer.

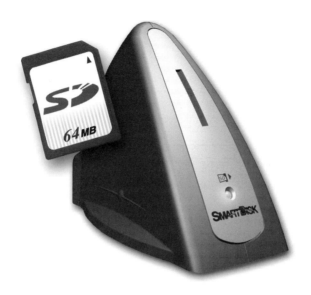

*Card readers are one of the easiest ways to transfer photos from the SD card to your computer.*

*Note:* There are subtle differences in the functionality of these two methods. For example, connecting the D50 to a compatible printer allows you to perform cropping before printing. However, when printing from the memory card, only "full frame" is available (unless the printer's software allows cropping).

*Note:* The various methods of direct printing do not support images saved in the NEF RAW format. If you select a NEF RAW picture in one of the direct printing options a warning message – REQUIRES JPEG PHOTO TAKEN BY D50—will be displayed on the LCD monitor screen. To print these images transfer them to a computer and print them directly from Nikon Picture Project 1.5 or later, Nikon View 6.2.6 or later, alternatively use the optional Nikon Capture 4.3 or later.

*Note:* If you shoot pictures using P, S, A, and M exposure modes with the intention of printing them without further modification then either choose Direct print from the Optimize Image menu, or select Custom and set the color mode to Ia (sRGB) or IIIa (sRGB) according to the subject.

**Linking the D50 with a Printer**

To connect the D50 to a PictBridge compatible printer in order to print pictures directly from the camera follow the four steps below:

• Set the USB option in the Setup Menu to PTP.

• Turn the printer ON and the camera OFF.

• Connect the printer to the camera using the supplied UC-E4 USB cord.

• Turn the camera ON and the PictBridge welcome screen will appear followed by the PictBridge playback display; a single image displayed at full screen size. You now have two further options: to print pictures individually, or in multiples (see below).

*Note:* It is essential that you make sure the camera battery is fully charged before starting direct printing from the camera. To be safe, particularly for protracted printing sessions power the camera with the accessory EH-5 AC adapter.

**PictBridge Playback Display**

Once you have open the PictBridge playback display as described above you can use the ⊙⊙ to scroll through the recorded pictures. To zoom in on the selected image press and hold the [ENTER] button. To view six thumbnail images at a time press the ⊠ button; you can use the ⊙⊙ to scroll through the displayed pictures, which highlights the selected picture with a yellow border frame. Press the ⊠ button to display the highlighted picture at full screen size.

## PictBridge Menu: Printing Pictures One at a Time

To print the individual photograph displayed via the Pict-Bridge playback display, press and release the [ENTER] button. This displays a Setup menu with the following options:

*Start Printing*—the selected picture is printed and the Pict-Bridge playback display will be shown once printing is finished. To cancel printing, press the [ENTER] button.

*Page Size*—The available page sizes for the selected printer will be displayed. Use the multi selector switch to select the required page size, and press ⊙ to return to the print menu.

*Number of Copies*—Press ⊙ to select the number of copies to be printed (maximum 99) and press ⊙ to return to the print menu.

*Border*—Press ⊙ to highlight one of the three options: Printer Default (uses default setting of selected printer), Print with Border (picture is printed with a white border), or No Border, and press ⊙ to return to the print menu.

*Time Stamp*—Press ⊙ to highlight one of the three options: Printer Default (uses default setting of selected printer), Print Time Stamp (picture is printed with the time and date of recording shown on the photograph), or No Time Stamp, and press ⊙ to return to the print menu.

*Cropping*—Press ⊙ to highlight one of the two options: Crop (picture is printed cropped as determined by the user) rotate the command dial to select the degree of cropping and use the multi selector switch to select the position of the crop. Once you have decided on the required crop press the [ENTER] button to return to the print menu. If you select No Cropping, the picture is printed full frame.

## PictBridge Menu: Printing Multiple Pictures

The D50 allows you to print multiple pictures from the Pict-Bridge menu as well as creating an index print (contact sheet) showing the JPEG images stored on the memory card as small thumbnail images. Press the 🔲 button and a menu with the following options will be displayed:

***Print Select***—selected pictures will be printed (see instructions below)

***Print (DPOF)***—pictures selected in the current DPOF print order will be printed (see instructions below)

**Note:** The Print Select option in the PictBridge menu should not be confused with the Print Set option within the Playback menu. Only the latter option allows you to print pictures from a DPOF compatible printer.

***Index Print***—up to a maximum of 265 pictures stored on the memory card in the JPEG format are printed as thumbnails to create an index print (see instructions below)

To print multiple pictures from the PictBridge menu highlight Print Select and press ⚬ to display a series of six thumbnail pictures. A yellow border frame will surround the currently selected picture; use the left and right arrows on the multi selector switch to scroll through the stored pictures and select the highlighted picture for printing by pressing ⚬ and a small printer icon will appear in the image area together with the figure 1, which indicates that one copy will be printed. If you press ⚬ again the figure will increase incrementally by one each time to show the number of copies that will be printed to a maximum of 99. Pressing ⚬ decreases the number of copies that will be printed. To deselect a picture press ⚬ until the printer icon disappears. Repeat this procedure for each image that you want to print. Once you have finished your selection press 🔲 to display the PictBridge setup menu, which has options for Page Size, Border, and Time Stamp (these operate as described above under Printing Pictures One at a Time).

To print the selected pictures highlight Start Printing and press ⚬ ; the PictBridge menu will be displayed once printing is finished.

**Playback Menu: Print Set - Digital Print Order Format (DPOF)**

If you are away from home, say on vacation, you can still produce prints from your digital files even if you do not have your own printer with you. The D50 supports Digital Print Order Format (DPOF) that, unlike PictBridge, embeds data in the image file that allows you to insert the memory card into any DPOF compatible home printer or commercial mini-lab printer, and get a set of prints of those images you want.

To select images for printing, open the Playback Menu and navigate to Print Set, then press ⊙ to select it. Highlight Select/set and press ⊙ to open the option. A series of six thumbnail images will displayed on the LCD monitor from the folder, or folders, selected in the Playback fldr menu; scroll through the images by pressing ⊙ . This action moves a yellow border frame to highlight the selected image (to view the image at full screen size press and hold ⊞ ). To select an image for printing press ⊙ and a small printer icon will appear in the image area together with the figure 1, which indicates that one copy will be printed. If you press ⊙ again the figure will increase incrementally by one each time to show the number of copies that will be printed. Pressing ⊙ decreases the number of copies that will be printed. To deselect a picture press ⊙ until the printer icon disappears. Repeat this procedure for each image that you want to print.

To confirm the printing instruction for the selected image(s) press ⊞ENTER , which returns you to the Print Set menu. This presents you with three options: Done, Data imprint, and Imprint Date.

Selecting the Data Imprint option will cause the shutter speed and lens aperture to be printed within the picture area of all images selected for printing; highlight the option and press ⊙ to activate it.

Selecting the Imprint Date option will cause the date of recording to be printed within the picture area of all images selected for printing; highlight the option and press ⊙ to activate it.

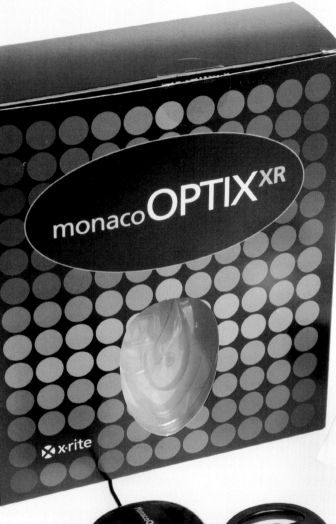
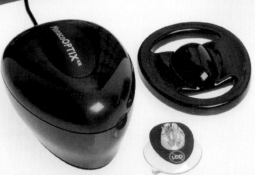

Finally, to complete and confirm the printing instruction for the selected image(s), and return to the Playback menu, highlight Done and press ⟲ .

**Index Print**
Highlight the Index Print option in the PictBridge menu and press ⟲ to select it. Six thumbnail images will be displayed with the currently select picture surrounded by a yellow border frame.

Press **ENTER** to display the PictBridge setup menu, which has options for Page Size, Border, and Time Stamp (these operate as described above under Printing Pictures One at a Time).

To print the pictures as a series of thumbnails highlight Start Printing and press ⟲ ; the PictBridge menu will be displayed once printing is finished.

**Error Messages**
During printing it is possible that a dialog box with the message—PRINT ERROR may appear. If this occurs check the cord connection between the camera and printer, and the printer settings according to the manufacturer's instructions. Once these checks have been completed either highlight Continue to resume printing, or Cancel to stop printing immediately without printing any more images.

*All digital imaging equipment renders color slightly differently. If you are getting prints that do not match your computer's or camera's monitor the MonacoOPTIX XR can help you to profile your equipment to assure accurate color fidelity. ©MAC Group.*

# Nikon Software

It is beyond the scope of this book to describe in detail the features and functions of Nikon's dedicated software, which can be obtained from one of the many Nikon Corporation web site pages that deal with them, so I have provided merely an overview. The D50 comes with a copy of Nikon PictureProject 1.5 Nikon's new browser application intended to replace Nikon View. I say intended because despite statements suggesting that Nikon View would be taken no further than version 6.0 Nikon has continued to update it to ensure compatibility with the many of the recent upgrades to Nikon Capture, although it does not support all of the new tools in version 4.3 of this application with NEF RAW files. However, it is unclear at the time of writing how much longer Nikon View will continue to be developed but the current iteration is at version 6.2.6, which was introduced to offer support to the D50!

I believe the continued availability and popularity of Nikon View is a clear indication of the shortcomings of PictureProject, and can be attributed to its far greater maturity as a piece of software, particularly in respect of its support for NEF RAW files, which is something that leaves PictureProject wanting. If you have not tried Nikon View I would strongly recommend that you do – after all it is free!

### Nikon Picture Project 1.5 and Nikon View 6.2.6

As explained, the D50 comes supplied with a copy of Nikon PictureProject 1.5, and updates are available free for download from Nikon's various support websites, as is Nikon View 6.2.6 (see page 229). Both applications control the transfer of images, either directly from the camera or from a card reader, and allow a number of preferences to be set, including file naming and numbering. Both of these also provide an image browsing capability to display images so you can review, sort, and edit them once they have been transferred to a computer.

As soon as the transfer is complete and images have been placed in the appropriate folder, the browser window will auto-launch and the last set of images to be imported will be displayed as a series of thumbnail pictures. Shooting data can be viewed in Nikon PictureProject by opening the View menu and selecting Display > List, or alternatively click on the List button in the bottom right corner of the main pane, the information for each image shown in the main pane will be displayed beside it. In Nikon View click on the Shooting Data tab: the information for the highlighted image (it will be highlighted by a selection frame) is then shown in a box that opens beneath the menu bar. Both applications allow you to search for other images in the directory tree shown to the left side of the main browser window.

PictureProject permits you to perform some very basic editing; click on the Edit button, this displays buttons to crop, rotate, and zoom the image, as well as a red-eye reduction tool. Opening the Photo Enhance menu reveals some further options, including tools for controlling Brightness, D-Lighting, Color Booster, Photo Effects, Sharpening, and Straightening.

By comparison Nikon View contains a restricted version of Nikon Editor, which allows you to use a limited number of tools and controls, including brightness, contrast, image size, sharpening (although no parameters are shown—just Off, Low, Medium, and High), and red-eye reduction (only available for JPEG files). Nikon View benefits from having further controls that permit exposure compensation of +/- 2EV, and modification of the white balance value (within the available presets) for NEF RAW files, which can be adjusted at any time. Plus NEF RAW files can then be saved as either 8-bit or16-bit TIFF files, as well as JPEG files.

*Note:* It is not possible to rescue grossly overexposed images using exposure compensation, as areas with burnt out high-lights will have no data for the application to work with.

*Note:* In practical terms, the range of exposure compensation for NEF files using Nikon Editor within Nikon View software is closer to – 1.5EV to +1EV, as changes beyond these limits can introduce unwanted artifacts.

**Nikon Capture 4.3**

Nikon Capture is a far more sophisticated application compared with Nikon PictureProject of Nikon View, as it permits a much greater level of image control and the ability to operate compatible cameras remotely. It is available as an optional extra, and has two distinct components: Nikon Editor and Nikon Camera Control. Nikon Editor is used to assist processing and enhancing of NEF and JPEG files, with the option of converting them to other formats, or opening them directly into another image-processing application, such as Adobe Photoshop. Nikon Camera Control allows full remote control of a D50 while the camera is connected to a computer via a UC-E4 USB cable. It also allows the direct transfer of images from the camera to a computer, effectively turning the computer hard drive in to a large volume memory card.

*Nikon Capture 4 Editor offers many features, including:*

- Advanced white balance control with the ability to select a specific color temperature, or sample from a gray point.

- Advanced NEF file control that permits attributes such as exposure compensation, sharpening, contrast, color mode, saturation, and hue to be modified after the exposure has been made, without affecting the original image data.

- The Image Dust Off feature, which compares an NEF file with a reference image taken with the same camera to help reduce the effects of any dust particles on the low-pass filter

- The D-Lighting tool, which emulates the dodge & burn techniques of traditional photographic printing to control highlight and shadow areas to produce a more balanced exposure

216

- A Color Noise Reduction tool, which minimizes the effect of random electronic noise that can occur, especially at high sensitivity settings

- An Edge Noise Reduction tool that accentuates the boundary between areas of the image to make them more distinct

- The Color Moiré Reduction feature helps to remove the effects of moiré, which can occur when an image contains areas with a very fine repeating pattern

- LCH Editor allows for control of Luminosity (overall lightness), Chroma (colour saturation), and Hue in separate channels

- Fisheye Lens tool converts images taken with the AF Fisheye-Nikkor DX 10.5mm f/2.8G lens so they appear as though they were taken using a conventional rectilinear lens with a diagonal angle-of-view equivalent to approximately 120º

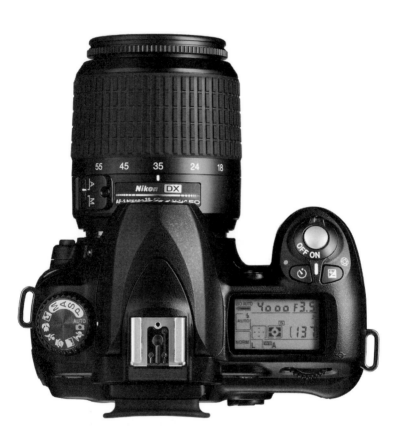

# Making the Most of Your D50

## Workflow

The steps in using film for photography are familiar to most people: load the camera, take the pictures, and then have someone else do the processing and printing for you. Shooting digitally introduces a number of new aspects to these procedures, thereby providing a far greater level of involvement on the part of a photographer, and thus control over the process. Therefore, it is essential to develop a routine to make sure you work in an efficient and effective way. You may wish to consider the following seven-point workflow as a general guide to establishing your own routine.

### *Preparation:*

• Familiarize yourself with the camera.

• Make sure the camera battery is charged and carry a spare.

• Consider the consequences of saving al your pictures to a single large capacity memory card should it be lost or become corrupted; reduce the risk of a catastrophic loss by spreading your pictures across two or three different memory cards.

• Format all memory cards in the camera in which they will be used as soon as you insert the card. Do use a card that has been formatted in another camera, or a computer.

⟡ *Available in either black or chrome, the Nikon D50 represents the latest in fine digital SLR cameras from Nikon—a leading optical and equipment manufacturer. Properly cared for, your camera will produce quality digital images and be a pleasure to use for years to come.*

***Shooting:***
- Adjust camera settings to match the requirements of your shoot; choose an appropriate image quality, size, and color space.

- et other camera controls such as metering, ISO, white balance, and autofocus according to the particular shooting conditions.

- Review images on the spot and make any adjustments you deem necessary. The histogram display is extremely useful for checking exposure values.

- Do not be in too much of a hurry to delete pictures unless they are obvious failures. It is often better to edit after the shoot rather than "on the fly."

***Transfer:***
- Use a card reader rather than connecting the camera directly to the computer. It is more reliable and reduces wear and tear on the camera.

- Before transferring images to your computer, designate a specific folder or folders in which the images will be stored so you know where to find them.

- Consider renaming files and assigning further information and key words to facilitate locating images at a later date.

- If your browser application permits you to assign general information to the image files during transfer (e.g. DNPR metadata) make sure you complete appropriate fields for image authorship and copyright.

***Edit and File:***
- Use a browser application to sort through your pictures.

- Print a contact sheet of small thumbnail images to help you decide which images to retain.

## Processing:

- Make copies of RAW files and save them to a working file format such as TIFF or Adobe Photoshop PSD.

- Do not use the JPEG format for processing.

- Make adjustments in an orderly and logical sequence starting with overall brightness, contrast, and color. Then make more local adjustments to correct problems or enhance the image.

- Save your adjusted file as a master copy to which you can then apply a crop, resizing, sharpening, and any other finishing touches appropriate to your output requirements.

## Archive:

- Data can become lost or corrupted at any time for a variety of reasons, so always make multiple back-up copies of your original files and the edited master copies.

- CDs have a limited capacity, so consider DVDs or an external hard drive.

## Display:

- We all shoot pictures for others to see and enjoy. Digital technology has expanded the possibilities of image display considerably; we can email pictures to family and friends, prepare digital slideshows, or post images to a website.

- Home printing in full color is now reliable, cost effective, and, achievable. Spend time to set up your system properly; calibrate your monitor and printer regularly, use an appropriate resolution for the print size you require, then choose paper type and finish accordingly.

# Camera Settings

The following table lists the settings on the D50 that can be adjusted in each shooting mode. It is important to note that the Digital Vari-Program Modes deny access to many significant camera controls, including metering, white balance, exposure compensation, and exposure bracketing.

| | AUTO | Portrait | Landscape | Child | Sports | Close-up | Night | P | S | A | M |
|---|---|---|---|---|---|---|---|---|---|---|---|
| **Shooting menu** | | | | | | | | | | | |
| Optimize Image [1] | | | | | | | | • | • | • | • |
| Long Exp. NR | • | • | • | • | • | • | • | • | • | • | • |
| Image Quality [1] | • | • | • | • | • | • | • | • | • | • | • |
| Image Size [1] | • | • | • | • | • | • | • | • | • | • | • |
| White Balance [1] | | | | | | | | • | • | • | • |
| ISO [1] | •[2] | •[2] | •[2] | •[2] | •[2] | •[2] | •[2] | • | • | • | • |
| **Other settings** | | | | | | | | | | | |
| Shooting mode [1] | • | • | • | • | • | • | • | • | • | • | • |
| Flexible program [1] | | | | | | | | • | | | |
| Autoexposure lock [1] | • | • | • | • | • | • | • | • | • | • | • |
| Exposure compensation [1] | | | | | | | | • | • | • | • |
| Flash sync mode | •[3] | •[3] | | •[3] | | •[3] | •[3] | •[1] | •[1] | •[1] | •[1] |
| **Custom settings** | | | | | | | | | | | |
| 1: Beep [4] | • | • | • | • | • | • | • | • | • | • | • |
| 2: Autofocus [4] | | | | | | | | • | • | • | • |
| 3: AF-Area Mode [4] | •[3] | •[3] | •[3] | •[3] | •[3] | •[3] | •[3] | • | • | • | • |
| 4: No SD Card? [4] | • | • | • | • | • | • | • | • | • | • | • |
| 5: Image Review [4] | • | • | • | • | | | | • | • | • | • |
| 6: Flash Level [1,4] | | | | | | | | • | • | • | • |
| 7: AF Assist [4] | • | • | | • | | • | • | • | • | • | • |
| 8: AF Area Illm [4] | • | • | • | • | • | • | • | • | • | • | • |
| 9: ISO Control [4] | • | • | • | • | • | • | • | | | | |
| 10: ISO Auto [4] | •[2] | •[2] | •[2] | •[2] | •[2] | •[2] | •[2] | • | • | • | • |
| 11: EV Step [4] | • | • | • | • | • | • | • | • | • | • | • |
| 12: BKT Set [1,4] | | | | | | | | • | • | • | • |
| 13: Metering [1,4] | | | | | | | | • | • | • | • |
| 14: AE-L/AF-L [4] | • | • | • | • | • | • | • | • | • | • | • |
| 15: AE Lock [4] | • | • | • | • | • | • | • | • | • | • | • |
| 16: Flash Mode [4] | | | | | | | | • | • | • | • |
| 17: Monitor Off [4] | • | • | • | • | • | • | • | • | • | • | • |
| 18: Meter Off [4] | • | • | • | • | • | • | • | • | • | • | • |
| 19: Self-Timer [4] | • | • | • | • | • | • | • | • | • | • | • |
| 20: Remote [4] | • | • | • | • | • | • | • | • | • | • | • |

*1 Reset with two-button reset*
*2 Available when OFF is selected for Custom Setting 9*
*3 Reset when mode dial rotated to new setting*
*4 Reset with R: Menu Reset*

# Troubleshooting

The D50 is a sophisticated electronic device capable of reporting a range of malfunctions and problems by way of indicators and error messages that appear in the viewfinder, control panel, and LCD Monitor. The following tables will assist you in finding a solution should one of these indicators or messages be displayed.

| Indicator | | Problem | Solution |
|---|---|---|---|
| **Control panel** | **View-finder** | | |
| 🔋 | 🔋 | Low battery spare battery | Ready a fully-charged |
| 🔋 (blinks) | 🔋 (blinks) | Battery exhausted | Replace battery |
| 🔋 (blinks) | | Camera can not detect battery | Insert battery |
| CLOCK (blinks) | | Camera clock is not set | Set camera clock |
| -E- | ⯒ (blinks) -E- | No memory card | Insert memory card |
| FuLL 0 (blinks) | FuLL 0 (blinks) | Memory insufficient to record further photos at current settings, or camera has run out of file or folder numbers | • Reduce quality or size • Delete photographs • Insert new memory card |
| FE E (blinks) | | Lens aperture ring is not locked at minimum aperture | Lock ring at minimum aperture (largest f/ number |
| F- - (blinks) | | No lens attached, or non-CPU lens attached | Attach CPU lens (IX - Nikkor excluded), or rotate mode dial to **M** end use lens aperture ring to set aperture |
| | ● (blinks) | Camera unable to focus using autotocus | Focus manually |

| Indicator | | | |
|---|---|---|---|
| Control panel | View-finder | Problem | Solution |
| **H I** | | Subject too bright; photo will be overexposed | • Choose lower sensitivity<br>• Use optional Neutral Density (ND) filter<br>• In mode<br>**S** Increase shutter speed<br>**A** Choose smaller aperture (larger f/-number) |
| **L o** | | Subject too dark, photo will be underexposed | • Choose higher sensitivity<br>• Use built-in ash<br>• In mode<br>**S** Lower shutter speed<br>**A** Choose larger aperture (smaller f/-number) |
| | ⚡<br>(blinks) | • Flash required for correct exposure (P, S, A, M modes)<br>• Flash has fired at full power ( ⚡ blinks for three seconds after flash fires | • Raise built-in ash<br><br>• Check photo in monitor; if underexposed, adjust settings and try again |
| ⚡<br>(blinks) | ⚡ | Speedlight that does not support i-TTL flash control attached and set to TTL | Change flash mode setting on optional Speed light |
| **bu L b**<br>(blinks) | **bu L b** selected in mode **M** and mode dial rotated to **S** | Change shutter speed or select mode M | |
| **- -**<br>(blinks) | - - selected in mode **M** and mode dial rotated to **S** | Change shutter speed or select mode M | |
| **E r r**<br>(blinks) | | Camera malfunction | Release shutter. If error persists or appears frequently consult with Nikon authorized service representative |

| Indicator | | | |
|---|---|---|---|
| Monitor | Control panel | Problem | Solution |
| NO CARD PRESENT | [- E -] | Camera cannot detect memory card | Turn camera off and confirm that card is correctly inserted |
| THIS CARD CAN NOT BE USED | [E HR] (blinks) | • Error accessing memory card<br><br>• Unable to create new folder<br>• Card has not been formatted for use with D50 | • Use Nikon-approved card<br>• Check that contacts are clean. If card is damaged contact retailer or Nikon representative<br>• Delete files or insert new memory card<br>Format memory card |
| CARD IS NOT FORMATTED | [F o r] (blinks) | Memory card has not been formatted for the D50 | Format memory card |
| FOLDER CONTAINS NO IMAGES | | • Memory card contains no images<br>• Current folder is empty | • Insert another card<br><br>• Set **Playback fldr** to **All** |
| FILE DOES NOT CONTAIN IMAGE DATA | | File has been created or modified using a computer or different make of camera, or file is corrupt | Delete file or reformat memory card |
| CARD IS LOCKED | [E HR] (blinks) | Memory card is locked (write protected) | Slide write-protect switch to "write" position |

## Reset Button

Operation of the D50 is totally dependent on electrical power. Occasionally, the camera may stop functioning properly, or display unusual characters or unexpected messages in the viewfinder and LCD displays. Such behavior is generally due to the effects of electrostatic charge. If this occurs, try switching the camera off, disconnecting it from its power supply (remove the EN-EL3/3a battery, or unplug the EH-5 AC adapter), then reconnect the power, and switch the camera on again.

If this fails to rectify the situation, press the Reset Button located on the base of the camera toward the left-hand end. It is recessed in the base-plate of the camera, so you will need the tip of a ballpoint pen or a paperclip to access it. This will also cause the internal clock to return to its default date setting of 2005:01:01, so you will have to re-enter the correct date and time.

## Approved Memory Cards

There are a plethora of memory cards on the market consequently Nikon has only tested and approved a limited number. According to the Nikon Corporation the following Secure Digital (SD) cards have been tested and approved for use with the D50:

| Manufacturer / Model | Capacity |
|---|---|
| SanDisk | 64MB, 128MB, 256MB, 512 MB and 1GB |
| SanDisk Ultra II | 512 MB* |
| Panasonic | 64MB, 128MB, 256MB, 512 MB and 1GB |
| Panasonic Super High Speed | 256MB*, 512 MB* and 1GB* |
| Panasonic Pro High Speed | 512 MB* and 1GB* |
| Toshiba (blue) | 64MB, 128MB, 256MB and 512MB |
| Toshiba (white) | 128MB*, 256MB* and 512MB* |

*These cards support a data transfer rate of 10MB/s or more, and are therefore better suited if you expect to shoot frequent, rapid sequences of pictures.*

226

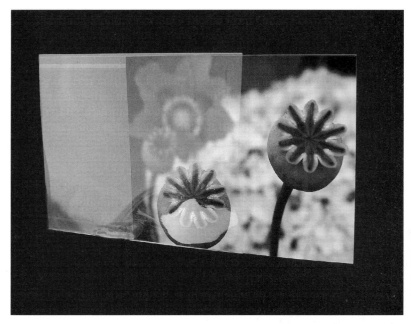

*While it is important to take good care of your camera gear, you should also protect your photographs from damage. Archival storage sleeves and boxes will ensure long life for your treasured pictures. ©Archival Methods*

However, solid-state flash memory technology is well established, so although Nikon will not guarantee operation with other brands and capacities of SD cards they will probably work, and you should not experience significant problems. However, if you are considering the use a memory card not listed in the table above it is probably best to check with the manufacturer for compatibility with the D50. If you need to do some troubleshooting it is recommended that you use an approved memory card, since card compatibility can be an issue.

**Note:** Multi Media cards (MMC) are not recommended and should not be used.

# Memory Card Capacity

The table below provides information on the approximate number of images that can be stored on a 256Mb memory card at the various image quality, and size settings available on the D50.

| Image Quality | Image Size | File Size (Mb)[1] | No of images[1] | Buffer Capcity[2] Long Exp. Nr – Off | Buffer Capcity[2] Long Exp. Nr – On |
|---|---|---|---|---|---|
| NEF (RAW) | - | 5.0 | 33 | 4 | 3 |
| JPEG Large | L | 2.9 | 70 | 9 | 7 |
| JPEG Large | M | 1.6 | 123 | 10 | 8 |
| JPEG Large | S | 0.8 | 258 | 19 | 17 |
| JPEG Normal | L | 1.5 | 137 | 12 | 10 |
| JPEG Normal | M | 0.8 | 233 | 16 | 14 |
| JPEG Normal | S | 0.4 | 464 | 27 | 25 |
| JPEG Basic | L | 0.8 | 258 | 19 | 17 |
| JPEG Basic | M | 0.4 | 423 | 27 | 25 |
| JPEG Basic | S | 0.2 | 770 | 49 | 47 |
| NEF + JPEG Basic | L | 5.83 | 29 | 4 | 3 |

[1]   *These figures are approximate, as the file size will vary according to the nature of the scene recorded and the make and model of the memory card.*

[2]   *These figures represent the maximum number of pictures that can be stored in the buffer memory. The actual number of pictures that can be taken may be lower depending on the status, of the buffer memory, and the make and model of the memory card.*

[3]   *This the total combined size for the NEF (RAW) and JPEG files.*

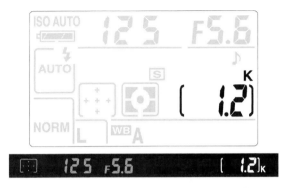

*If, at the current settings for image quality and size, the memory card has sufficient capacity to record 1000 pictures or more, the number of remain exposures will be shown in thousands but rounded down to the nearest 100. For example if the card could store a further 1250 exposures the exposure counter display in the control panel will show 1.2K.*

## Web Support

Nikon maintains product support, and provides further information on-line at a variety of web sites. To access these visit:

**http://www.nikon.com**

For specific technical support and downloads of software and camera firmware visit:

**http://www.nikonusa.com for North America**

**http://www.europe-nikon.com/support** for most European countries

**http://www.nikon-asia.com** for Asia, Oceania, Middle East, and Africa

# Glossary

**AA**

Auto aperture. Refers to a Nikon flash mode in which the flash level is automatically adjusted for aperture.

**aberration**

An optical flaw in a lens that causes the image to be distorted or unclear.

**AF-D**

AF Nikkor lenses that communicate the distance of the focused subject to a compatible camera body in order to improve the accuracy of exposure calculations for both ambient light and flash. (AF-G, AF-I, and AF-S lenses also perform this function.) AF-D lenses are focused by a motor mounted in the camera body.

**AF-G**

AF Nikkor lenses that lack a conventional aperture ring. They are only compatible with those cameras that permit the aperture to be set from the camera body.

**AF-I**

The first series of AF Nikkor lenses to have an internal focusing motor.

**AF-S**

AF Nikkor lenses that use a silent wave focusing motor mounted within the lens. The technology used in AF-S lenses permits faster and more responsive automatic focusing as compared to the AF-I and AF-D lenses.

**AI**

Automatic Indexing.

**AI-S**

Nikon F-mount lens bayonet for manual focus Nikkor lenses. They have a small notch milled out of the bayonet ring.

**angle of view**

The area seen by a lens, usually measured in degrees across the diagonal of the film frame.

**anti-aliasing**

A technique that reduces or eliminates the jagged appearance of lines or edges in an image.

**aperture**

The opening in the lens that allows light to enter the camera. Aperture is usually described as an f/number. The higher the f/number, the smaller the aperture; the lower the f/number, the larger the aperture.

**Aperture-Priority mode**

A type of automatic exposure in which you manually select the aperture and the camera automatically selects the shutter speed.

**artifact**

Information that is not part of the scene but appears in the image due to technology. Artifacts can occur in film or digital images and include increased grain, flare, static marks, color flaws, noise, etc.

**artificial light**

Usually refers to any light source that doesn't exist in nature, such as incandescent, fluorescent, and other manufactured lighting.

**astigmatism**

An optical defect that occurs when an off-axis point is brought to focus as sagittal and tangential lines rather than a point.

**automatic exposure**

When the camera measures light and makes the adjustments necessary to create proper image density on sensitized media.

**automatic flash**

An electronic flash unit that reads light reflected off a subject (from either a preflash or the actual flash exposure), then shuts itself off as soon as ample light has reached the sensitized medium.

**automatic focus**

When the camera automatically adjusts the lens elements to sharply render the subject.

**available light**

The amount of illumination at a given location that applies to natural and artificial light sources but not those supplied specifically for photography. It is also called existing light or ambient light.

**backlight**

Light that projects toward the camera from behind the subject.

**backup**

A copy of a file or program made to ensure that, if the original is lost or damaged, the necessary information is still intact.

**barrel distortion**
A defect in the lens that makes straight lines curve outward away from the middle of the image.

**bit**
Binary digit. This is the basic unit of binary computation. See also, byte.

**bit depth**
The number of bits per pixel that determines the number of colors the image can display. Eight bits per pixel is the minimum requirement for a photo-quality color image.

**bounce light**
Light that reflects off of another surface before illuminating the subject.

**bracketing**
A sequence of pictures taken of the same subject but varying one or more exposure settings, manually or automatically, between each exposure.

**brightness**
A subjective measure of illumination. See also, luminance.

**buffer**
Temporarily stores data so that other programs, on the camera or the computer, can continue to run while data is in transition.

**built-in flash**
A flash that is permanently attached to the camera body. The built-in flash will pop up and fire in low-light situations when using the camera's automated exposure settings.

**built-in meter**
A light measuring device that is incorporated into the camera body.

**bulb**
A camera setting that allows the shutter to stay open as long as the shutter release is depressed.

**byte**
A single group of eight bits that is processed as one unit. See also, bit.

**card reader**
Device that connects to your computer and enables quick and easy download of images from memory card to computer.

**CCD**
Charge Coupled Device. This is a common digital camera sensor type that is sensitized by applying an electrical charge to the sensor prior to its exposure to light. It converts light energy into an electrical impulse.

**chromatic aberration**
Occurs when light rays of different colors are focused on different planes, causing colored halos around objects in the image.

**chrominance**
Hue and saturation information.

**chrominance noise**
A form of artifact that appears as a random scattering of densely packed colored "grain." See also, luminance and noise.

**close-up**
A general term used to describe an image created by closely focusing on a subject.

Often involves the use of special lenses or extension tubes. Also, an automated exposure setting that automatically selects a large aperture (not available with all cameras).

**CLS**
Creative Lighting System. This is a flash control system that Nikon introduced with its SB-800 and SB-600 Speedlights. See also, Speedlight.

**CMOS**
Complementary Metal Oxide Semiconductor. Like CCD sensors, this sensor type converts light into an electrical impulse. CMOS sensors are similar to CCDs, but allow individual processing of pixels, are less expensive to produce, and use less power. See also, CCD.

**CMYK mode**
Cyan, magenta, yellow, and black. This mode is typically used in image-editing applications when preparing an image for printing.

**color balance**
The average overall color in a reproduced image. How a digital camera interprets the color of light in a scene so that white or neutral gray appear neutral.

**color cast**
A colored hue over the image often caused by improper lighting or incorrect white balance settings. Can be produced intentionally for creative effect.

**color space**
A mapped relationship between colors and computer data about the colors.

**CompactFlash (CF) card**
One of the most widely used removable memory cards.

**complementary colors**
In theory: any two colors of light that, when combined, emit all known light wavelengths, resulting in white light. Also, it can be any pair of dye colors that absorb all known light wavelengths, resulting in black.

**compression**
Method of reducing file size through removal of redundant data, as with the JPEG file format.

**contrast**
The difference between two or more tones in terms of luminance, density, or darkness.

**contrast filter**
A colored filter that lightens or darkens the monotone representation of a colored area or object in a black-and-white photograph.

**CPU**
Central Processing Unit. This is the "brains" of a computer or a lens that perform principle computational functions.

**critical focus**
The most sharply focused plane within an image.

**cropping**
The process of extracting a portion of the image area. If this portion of the image is enlarged, resolution is subsequently lowered.

**dedicated flash**
An electronic flash unit that talks with the camera, communicating things such as flash illumination, lens focal length, subject distance, and sometimes flash status.

**default**
Refers to various factory-set attributes or features, in this case of a camera, that can be changed by the user but can, as desired, be reset to the original factory settings.

**depth of field**
The image space in front of and behind the plane of focus that appears acceptably sharp in the photograph.

**diaphragm**
A mechanism that determines the size of the lens opening that allows light to pass into the camera when taking a photo.

**digital zoom**
The cropping of the image at the sensor to create the effect of a telephoto zoom lens. The camera interpolates the image to the original resolution. However, the result is not as sharp as an image created with an optical zoom lens because the cropping of the image reduced the available sensor resolution.

**diopter**
A measurement of the refractive power of a lens. Also, it may be a supplementary lens that is defined by its focal length and power of magnification.

**download**
The transfer of data from one device to another, such as from camera to computer or computer to printer.

**dpi**
Dots per inch. Used to define the resolution of a printer, this term refers to the number of dots of ink that a printer can lay down in an inch.

**DPOF**
Digital Print Order Format. A feature that enables the camera to supply data about the printing order of image files and the supplementary data contained within them. This feature can only be used in conjunction with a DPOF compatible printer.

**D-TTL**
A flash control system that relies on a series of pre-flashes to determine the output required from a Nikon Speedlight. The system does not monitor the flash output during actual exposure. See also, Speedlight.

**D-type Nikkor**
A series of lenses that have a built-in CPU that is used to communicate the focus distance information to the camera body, improving the accuracy of exposure measurement.

**DX**
Nikkor lenses designed specifically for the Nikon DX format sensor.

**dye sublimation printer**
Creates color on the printed page by vaporizing inks that then solidify on the page.

**ED glass**
Extra-low Dispersion glass. Developed by Nikon, this glass was incorporated into many of their camera lenses to reduce the effects of chro-

matic aberration. See also, chromatic aberration.

### electronic flash
A device with a glass or plastic tube filled with gas that, when electrified, creates an intense flash of light. Also called a strobe. Unlike a flash bulb, it is reusable.

### electronic rangefinder
A system that utilizes the AF technology built into a camera to provide a visual confirmation that focus has been achieved. It can operate in either manual or AF focus modes.

### EV
Exposure Value. A number that quantifies the amount of light within an scene, allowing you to determine the relative combinations of aperture and shutter speed to accurately reproduce the light levels of that exposure.

### EXIF
Exchangeable Image File Format. This format is used for storing an image file's interchange information.

### exposure
When light enters the camera and reacts with the sensitized medium. The term can also refer to the amount of light that strikes the light sensitive medium.

### exposure meter
See light meter.

### extension tube
A hollow metal ring that can be fitted between the camera and lens. It increases the distance between the optical center of the lens and the

sensor and decreases the minimum focus distance of the lens.

### FAT
File Allocation Table. This is a method used by computer operating systems to keep track of files stored on the hard drive.

### file format
The form in which digital images are stored and recorded, e.g., JPEG, RAW, TIFF, etc.

### filter
Usually a piece of plastic or glass used to control how certain wavelengths of light are recorded. A filter absorbs selected wavelengths, preventing them from reaching the light sensitive medium. Also, software available in image-processing computer programs can produce special filter effects.

### FireWire
A high speed data transfer standard that allows outlying accessories to be plugged and unplugged from the computer while it is turned on. Some digital cameras and card readers use FireWire to connect to the computer. FireWire transfers data faster than USB. See also, Mbps.

### firmware
Software that is permanently incorporated into a hardware chip. All computer-based equipment, including digital cameras, use firmware of some kind.

### flare
Unwanted light streaks or rings that appear in the

viewfinder, on the recorded image, or both. It is caused by extraneous light entering the camera during shooting. Diffuse flare is uniformly reflected light that can lower the contrast of the image. Zoom lenses are susceptible to flare because they are comprised of many elements. Filters can also increase flare. Use of a lens hood can often reduce this undesirable effect.

### focal length
When the lens is focused on infinity, it is the distance from the optical center of the lens to the focal plane.

### focal plane
The plane on which a lens forms a sharp image. Also, it may be the film plane or sensor plane.

### focus
An optimum sharpness or image clarity that occurs when a lens creates a sharp image by converging light rays to specific points at the focal plane. The word also refers to the act of adjusting the lens to achieve optimal image sharpness.

### FP high-speed sync
Focal Plane high-speed sync. Some digital cameras emulate high shutter speeds by switching the camera sensor on and off rather than moving the shutter blades or curtains that cover it. This allows flash units to be synchronized at shutter speeds higher than the standard sync speed. In this flash mode, the level of flash output is reduced and, consequently, the shooting range is reduced.

### f/stop

The size of the aperture or diaphragm opening of a lens, also referred to as f/number or stop. The term stands for the ratio of the focal length (f) of the lens to the width of its aperture opening. (f/1.4 = wide opening and f/22 = narrow opening.) Each stop up (lower f/number) doubles the amount of light reaching the sensitized medium. Each stop down (higher f/number) halves the amount of light reaching the sensitized medium.

### full-frame

The maximum area covered by the sensitized medium.

### full-sized sensor

A sensor in a digital camera that has the same dimensions as a 35mm film frame (24 x 36 mm).

### gigabyte (GB)

Just over one billion bytes.

### GN

See guide number.

### gray card

A card used to take accurate exposure readings. It typically has a white side that reflects 90% of the light and a gray side that reflects 18%.

### gray scale

A successive series of tones ranging between black and white, which have no color.

### guide number (GN)

A number used to quantify the output of a flash unit. It is derived by using this formula: GN = aperture x distance. Guide numbers are expressed

for a given ISO film speed in either feet or meters.

### hard drive

A contained storage unit made up of magnetically sensitive disks.

### histogram

A graphic representation of image tones.

### hot shoe

An electronically connected flash mount on the camera body. It enables direct connection between the camera and an external flash, and synchronizes the shutter release with the firing of the flash.

### icon

A symbol used to represent a file, function, or program.

### IF

Internal Focusing. This Nikkor lens system shifts a group of elements within the lens to acquire focus more quickly without changing the overall length of the lens (as occurs with conventional, helical focusing mechanisms).

### image-processing program

Software that allows for image alteration and enhancement.

### infinity

In photographic terms, the theoretical most distant point of focus.

### interpolation

Process used to increase image resolution by creating new pixels based on existing pixels. The software intelligently looks at existing pixels and creates new pixels to fill the gaps and achieve a higher resolution.

### IS

Image Stabilization. This is a technology that reduces camera shake and vibration. It is used in lenses, binoculars, camcorders, etc.

### ISO

From ISOS (Greek for equal), a term for industry standards from the International Organization for Standardization. When an ISO number is applied to film, it indicates the relative light sensitivity of the recording medium. Digital sensors use film ISO equivalents, which are based on enhancing the data stream or boosting the signal.

### i-TTL

A Nikon TTL flash control system that has a refined monitor pre-flash sequence and offers improved flash exposure control. See also, TTL.

### JFET

Junction Field Effect Transistor, which are used in digital cameras to reduce the total number of transistors and minimize noise.

### JPEG

Joint Photographic Experts Group. This is a lossy compression file format that works with any computer and photo software. JPEG examines an image for redundant information and then removes it. It is a variable compression format because the amount of leftover data depends on the detail in the photo and the amount of compression. At low compression/high quality, the loss of data has a negligible effect on the photo. However, JPEG should not be used as a working format—the file should be reopened and saved in a format such as TIFF, which does not compress the image.

### kilobyte (KB)
Just over one thousand bytes.

### latitude
The acceptable range of exposure (from under to over) determined by observed loss of image quality.

### LBCAST
Lateral Buried Charge Accumulator and Sensing Transistor array. This is an array that converts received light into a digital signal, attaching an amplification circuit to each pixel of the imaging sensor.

### LCD
Liquid Crystal Display, which is a flat screen with two clear polarizing sheets on either side of a liquid crystal solution. When activated by an electric current, the LCD causes the crystals to either pass through or block light in order to create a colored image display.

### LED
Light Emitting Diode. It is a signal often employed as an indicator on cameras as well as on other electronic equipment.

### lens
A piece of optical glass on the front of a camera that has been precisely calibrated to allow focus.

### lens hood
Also called a lens shade. This is a short tube that can be attached to the front of a lens

to reduce flare. It keeps undesirable light from reaching the front of the lens and also protects the front of the lens.

### light meter
Also called an exposure meter, it is a device that measures light levels and calculates the correct aperture and shutter speed.

### lithium-ion
A popular battery technology (sometimes abbreviated to Li-ion) that is not prone to the charge memory effects of nickel-cadmium (Ni-Cd) batteries, or the low temperature performance problems of alkaline batteries.

### lossless
Image compression in which no data is lost.

### lossy
Image compression in which data is lost and, thereby, image quality is lessened. This means that the greater the compression, the lesser the image quality.

### low-pass filter
A filter designed to remove elements of an image that correspond to high-frequency data, such as sharp edges and fine detail, to reduce the effect of moiré. See also, moiré.

### luminance
A term used to describe directional brightness. It can also be used as luminance noise, which is a form of noise that appears as a sprinkling of black "grain." See also, brightness, chrominance, and noise.

### Mac
Macintosh. This is the brand

name for computers produced by Apple Computer, Inc.

### macro lens
A lens designed to be at top sharpness over a flat field when focused at close distances and reproduction ratios up to 1:1.

### main light
The primary or dominant light source. It influences texture, volume, and shadows.

### Manual exposure mode
A camera operating mode that requires the user to determine and set both the aperture and shutter speed. This is the opposite of automatic exposure.

### Mbps
Megabits per second. This unit is used to describe the rate of data transfer. See also, megabit.

### megabit
One million bits of data. See also, bit.

### megabyte (MB)
Just over one million bytes.

### megapixel
A million pixels.

### memory
The storage capacity of a hard drive or other recording media.

### memory card
A solid state removable storage medium used in digital devices. They can store still images, moving images, or sound, as well as related file data. There are several different types, including Compact-Flash, SmartMedia, and xD, or

Sony's proprietary Memory Stick, to name a few. Individual card capacity is limited by available storage as well as by the size of the recorded data (determined by factors such as image resolution and file format). See also, CompactFlash (CF) card, file format.

**menu**
A listing of features, functions, or options displayed on a screen that can be selected and activated by the user.

**microdrive**
A removable storage medium with moving parts. They are miniature hard drives based on the dimensions of a CompactFlash Type II card. Microdrives are more susceptible to the effects of impact, high altitude, and low temperature than solid-state cards are. See also, memory card.

**middle gray**
Halfway between black and white, it is an average gray tone with 18% reflectance. See also, gray card.

**midtone**
The tone that appears as medium brightness, or medium gray tone, in a photographic print.

**mode**
Specified operating conditions of the camera or software program.

**moiré**
Occurs when the subject has more detail than the resolution of the digital camera can capture. Moiré appears as a wavy pattern over the image.

**MOSFET**
Metal Oxide Semiconductor Field Effect Transistor, which is used as an amplifier in digital cameras.

**NEF**
Nikon Electronic File. This is Nikon's proprietary RAW file format, used by Nikon digital cameras. In order to process and view NEF files in your computer, you will need Nikon View (version 6.1 or newer) and Nikon Capture (version 4.1 or newer).

**Nikkor**
The brand name for lenses manufactured by Nikon Corporation.

**noise**
The digital equivalent of grain. It is often caused by a number of different factors, such as a high ISO setting, heat, sensor design, etc. Though usually undesirable, it may be added for creative effect using an image-processing program. See also, chrominance noise and luminance.

**normal lens**
See standard lens.

**operating system (OS)**
The system software that provides the environment within which all other software operates.

**overexposed**
When too much light is recorded with the image, causing the photo to be too light in tone.

**pan**
Moving the camera to follow a moving subject. When a slow shutter speed is used,

this creates an image in which the subject appears sharp and the background is blurred.

**PC**
Personal Computer. Strictly speaking, a computer made by IBM Corporation. However, the term is commonly used to refer to any IBM compatible computer.

**perspective**
The effect of the distance between the camera and image elements upon the perceived size of objects in an image. It is also an expression of this three-dimensional relationship in two dimensions.

**pincushion distortion**
A flaw in a lens that causes straight lines to bend inward toward the middle of an image.

**pixel**
Derived from picture element. A pixel is the base component of a digital image. Every individual pixel can have a distinct color and tone.

**plug-in**
Third-party software created to augment an existing software program.

**polarization**
An effect achieved by using a polarizing filter. It minimizes reflections from non-metallic surfaces like water and glass and saturates colors by removing glare. Polarization often makes skies appear bluer at 90 degrees to the sun. The term also applies to the above effects simulated by a polarizing software filter.

**pre-flashes**

A series of short duration, low intensity flash pulses emitted by a flash unit immediately prior to the shutter opening. These flashes help the TTL light meter assess the reflectivity of the subject. See also, TTL.

**Program mode**
In Program exposure mode, the camera selects a combination of shutter speed and aperture automatically.

**RAM**
Stands for Random Access Memory, which is a computer's memory capacity, directly accessible from the central processing unit.

**RAW**
An image file format that has little or no internal processing applied by the camera. It contains 12-bit color information, a wider range of data than 8-bit formats such as JPEG.

**RAW+JPEG**
An image file format that records two files per capture; one RAW file and one JPEG file.

**rear curtain sync**
A feature that causes the flash unit to fire just prior to the shutter closing. It is used for creative effect when mixing flash and ambient light.

**red-eye reduction**
A feature that causes the flash to emit a brief pulse of light just before the main flash fires. This helps to reduce the effect of retinal reflection.

**resolution**
The amount of data available for an image as applied to

image size. It is expressed in pixels or megapixels, or sometimes as lines per inch on a monitor or dots per inch on a printed image.

**RGB mode**
Red, Green, and Blue. This is the color model most commonly used to display color images on video systems, film recorders, and computer monitors. It displays all visible colors as combinations of red, green, and blue. RGB mode is the most common color mode for viewing and working with digital files onscreen.

**saturation**
The intensity or richness of a hue or color.

**SD (Secure Digital) card**
A flash memory card that is much smaller and lighter than CF (CompactFlash) cards; SD cards have metal connector contacts, instead of pins-and-plugs, so they aren't as prone to damage during handling compared with CF cards.

**sharp**
A term used to describe the quality of an image as clear, crisp, and perfectly focused, as opposed to fuzzy, obscure, or unfocused.

**short lens**
A lens with a short focal length—a wide-angle lens. It produces a greater angle of view than you would see with your eyes.

**shutter**
The apparatus that controls the amount of time during which light is allowed to reach the sensitized medium.

**Shutter-priority mode**
An automatic exposure mode in which you manually select the shutter speed and the camera automatically selects the aperture.

**slow sync**
A flash mode in which a slow shutter speed is used with the flash in order to allow low-level ambient light to be recorded by the sensitized medium.

**SLR**
Single-lens reflex. A camera with a mirror that reflects the image entering the lens through a pentaprism or pentamirror onto the viewfinder screen. When you take the picture, the mirror reflexes out of the way, the focal plane shutter opens, and the image is recorded.

**small-format sensor**
In a digital camera, this sensor is physically smaller than a 35mm frame of film. The result is that standard 35mm focal lengths act like longer lenses because the sensor sees an angle of view smaller than that of the lens.

**Speedlight**
The brand name of flash units produced by Nikon Corporation.

**standard lens**
Also known as a normal lens, this is a fixed-focal-length lens usually in the range of 45 to 55mm for 35mm format (or the equivalent range for small-format sensors). In contrast to wide-angle or telephoto lenses, a standard lens views a realistically proportionate perspective of a scene.

**stop down**
To reduce the size of the diaphragm opening by using a higher f/number.

**stop up**
To increase the size of the diaphragm opening by using a lower f/number.

**strobe**
Abbreviation for stroboscopic. An electronic light source that produces a series of evenly spaced bursts of light.

**synchronize**
Causing a flash unit to fire simultaneously with the complete opening of the camera's shutter.

**telephoto effect**
When objects in an image appear closer than they really are through the use of a telephoto lens.

**telephoto lens**
A lens with a long focal length that enlarges the subject and produces a narrower angle of view than you would see with your eyes.

**thumbnail**
A miniaturized representation of an image file.

**TIFF**
Tagged Image File Format. This popular digital format uses lossless compression.

**tripod**
A three-legged stand that stabilizes the camera and eliminates camera shake caused by body movement or vibration. Tripods are usually adjustable for height and angle.

**TTL**
Through-the-Lens, i.e. TTL metering.

**USB**
Universal Serial Bus. This interface standard allows outlying accessories to be plugged and unplugged from the computer while it is turned on. USB 2.0 enables high-speed data transfer.

**vignetting**
A reduction in light at the edge of an image due to use of a filter or an inappropriate lens hood for the particular lens.

**viewfinder screen**
The ground glass surface on which you view your image.

**VR**
Vibration Reduction. This technology is used in such photographic accessories as a VR lens.

**wide-angle lens**
A lens that produces a greater angle of view than you would see with your eyes, often causing the image to appear stretched. See also, short lens.

**Wi-Fi**
Wireless Fidelity, a technology that allows for wireless networking between one Wi-Fi compatible product and another.

**zoom lens**
A lens that can be adjusted to cover a wide range of focal lengths.

# Index

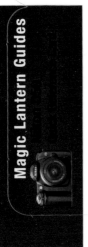

# Magic Lantern Guides

## Camera Operation Shortcuts

• **Set Exposure Mode:**
Rotate Mode Dial to P, A, S, or M.

• **Set Sensitivity (ISO Equivalent):**
Press/hold ISO button, rotate command dial.

• **Set Metering Mode:**
Open CS menu, select CS-13, select
⊠ = Matrix, ◉ = Center, ⊡ = Spot

• **Set Shooting Mode:**
Press/hold ⊕ button, rotate command dial.
⑤ = Single, ⬛ = Continuous

• **Set Self-timer/Remote Mode:**
Press/hold ⊕ button, rotate command dial.
⊙ = Self Timer, ⊶⬛ = Remote, Delayed
Release, ⬛ = Remote, Immediate Release

• **Set White Balance:**
Press/hold WB button, rotate command dial.

• **Set Bracketing:**
Open CS menu, select CS-12, select
Off, AE& flash, or WB.

• **Set Autofocus Mode:**
Open CS menu, select CS-2, select AF-A
(auto), AF-S (single-servo) or AF-C (continuous-servo).

• **Set Autofocus Area Mode:**
Open CS menu, select CS-3, select Single,
Dynamic, or Closest Subject.

• **Set Image Quality/Size:**
Press/hold QUAL button, rotate command
dial, select RAW, JPEG Fine,
Norm, Basic (L, M, or S), or RAW + Basic L.

• **Review Images:**
Single: Press ▶ button
Multiple: Press ▶ button, then press ⊞
button = x4, press ⊞ again = x9.

• **View Help Function:**
Highlight required item in CS menu,
press/hold ⊛ button.

• **Restore Default Settings:**
Press/hold BKT button and ⊙ button for
+2 seconds.

## Using Flash

• **Set Flash Sync Mode:**
In P, A, S, or M mode—Press/hold ⚡ button,
rotate command dial.
⬛ = Front,  ⬛ = Redeye Reduction
⬛ = Slow,  ⬛ = Slow + Redeye Reduction,
⬛ = Rear,  ⬛ = Slow + Rear

• **Flash Sync Speed:**
P = 1/500–1/60s
A = 1/500–1/60s
S = 1/500–30s
M = 1/500–30s
All modes = 1/500–30s with Slow, Slow +
Redeye Reduction, and Rear

• **Built-in Flash Shooting Range:**

| ISO 200 | ISO 800 | Range |
|---------|---------|-------|
| f/2 | f/4 | 3'3"–24'7"/1–7.7m |
| f/4 | f/8 | 2'–12'6"/0.6–3.8m |
| f/8 | f/16 | 2'–6'3"/0.6–1.9m |
| f/16 | f/32 | 2'–2'11"/0.6–0.9m |

• **Set Flash Exposure Compensation:**
Activate flash, press/hold ⚡ + ⊞ buttons,
rotate command dial (+1 to –3EV)

## Camera Menus

**• ▶ Playback Menu:**
Delete, Playback Folder, Rotate Tall, Slide Show, Print Set, Small Picture

**• ▣ Shooting Menu:**
Optimize, Long Exposure NR, Image Quality, Image Size, WB, ISO

**• ✎ Custom Settings Menu:**
**Simple (7 options):** Menu Reset, Beep, Autofocus, AF-area mode, No SD card, Image Review, Flash level

**Detailed (+14 options):** AF Assist, AF Area illumination, ISO Control, ISO Auto, EV Step, Bracket set, Metering, AE-L/AF-L, AE lock, Flash Mode, Monitor Off, Meter Off, Self Timer, Remote.

**• ⚙ Setup Menu:**
**Simple (8 options):** Format, CSM/Setup, Date, LCD, Brightness, Video Mode, Language, Image Comment, USB,

**Detailed (+6 options):** Folders, File No, Mirror Lockup, Dust Ref Photo, Firmware Version, Image Rotation

## Warning Messages

**FE E** blinks: Lens aperture not set to minimum value.
**F - -** blinks: No lens attached or non-CPU lens attached.
**E r r** blinks: Non-specific camera malfunction.

**• Battery Warning:**
⬛▮: Battery power is low.
⬛▮ blinks: Battery is exhausted.

**• Exposure Warnings:**
**H i** : Subject too bright, photo will be over-exposed.
**L o** : Subject too dark, photo will be under-exposed.
**✦** blinks: Use flash.
Highlights blink in playback image: Highlights are overexposed.

**• Card Warnings:**
**[F o r]** : Memory card not formatted.
**-E-** : Camera cannot detect memory card.
**Full** : Memory card is full.
**[CHR]** : Memory card cannot be accessed.

## Troubleshooting

**• Camera does not acquire focus:**
Switch to manual focus.

**• Consistent over- or underexposure:**
Confirm no exposure compensation is set.

**• Pictures are blurred:**
Shutter speed too slow. Use faster speed and/or tripod.

**• Camera ceases to function properly:**
Switch off, remove battery and replace it, switch on. If problem persists press the reset button on camera base.

**• Flash pictures underexposed:**
Reduce shooting range, use larger lens aperture, or higher ISO.

**• Random dark spots in image:**
Dust or dirt particles on the low pass filter.

**• Shutter does not operate:**
Camera has not acquired focus in AF-S (Single-servo) mode.